50 Ready-To-Use Assemblies

For Niall, Beth,
and the next generation . . .

50 Ready-to-Use Assemblies

DAVID BURT

EASTBOURNE

First published 2003
New edition 2006
1 2 3 4 5 6 Print/Year 09 08 07 06

Unless otherwise indicated, biblical quotations are from
the New International Version © 1973, 1978, 1984
by the International Bible Society.

ISBN 1 84291 323 9
13–ISBN: 978–1–842913–23–9

Cover design by
pinnaclecreative.co.uk

Published by
Kingsway Communications Ltd
Lottbridge Drove, Eastbourne, BN23 6NT, England.
Email: books@kingsway.co.uk

Printed in the USA

CONTENTS

PART ONE: PERSONAL, SOCIAL AND MORAL DEVELOPMENT

PART TWO: CULTURAL DEVELOPMENT

PART THREE: SPIRITUAL DEVELOPMENT

ACKNOWLEDGEMENTS

I want to say a big thanks to all the people who have offered me their time, wisdom and creativity in the preparation and writing of this book. To try and name them all individually is a difficult job, and also potentially embarrassing if I miss anyone out! But I'll give it a go anyway . . .

Muchos gracias to Dave, Richard, Tom, Ben, Keith, James, Emily, Nick, John, Chris, Lor and to everyone at Cranleigh Baptist Church for their support—you're all beautiful (well, except Ben, who has ridiculously large ears!).

If I've forgotten anyone, please let me know and I promise I will punish myself suitably and severely.

WHY DO ASSEMBLIES?

I recently passed that depressing threshold in life, when you suddenly realise that you've lived more years since leaving school than when you were there! It comes as a particular shock if, like me, you are imbued with youthful good looks and a generally young outlook on life. (All right, that's not strictly true, but you get the point.) Although it's a good number of years since I gleefully hopped, skipped and jumped out of the school gates for the last time, clutching a few reasonable 'O' level passes, I can vividly recall much of my life at school.

One thing that certainly doesn't escape my recollection is the daily dirge of turgidity, otherwise known as assembly! I cannot begin to explain to you how pitiful our assemblies were, and it sends a chill down my spine as I conjure up images of being totally bored assembly fodder.

It was with these early images in mind that the idea of doing a book of assembly outlines came up. But could it really be possible to raise an assembly above the usual rigid grind to being a truly positive experience? I began my research by asking various friends and colleagues in teaching and youth work this simple question: 'What's the point of doing an assembly?'

As you can imagine I got a good variety of answers ranging from the ridiculous to the sublime. Some said the right things, intimating we need to positively encourage and challenge the students with various issues. One more cynically suggested that the main point of doing an assembly was to give staff time to do their photocopying! One friend showed me a great quotation from the then DfEE (now DfES), which states: 'Teachers must demonstrate that they plan opportunities to contribute to pupils' personal, spiritual, moral, social and cultural development' (Bd DfEE circular 4/98).

What better forum than an assembly to address some of these key issues in fun and innovative ways? Instead of just doing what we think a school needs, let's support them by helping them achieve one of their key directives. The five areas of development listed in this quotation subsequently formed the structural backbone of this book. I have tried as best I can to group the illustrations, though of course many fit comfortably into two or more areas.

From the outset it is worth stating that although this book has been written with a Christian slant, I have attempted to make it possible to use as a resource by any schoolteachers as well as visiting Christian speakers. Whereas many of the illustrations make an obvious spiritual point, others cover more social and moral questions, and not all the spiritual ones necessarily use an overt evangelistic message.

If churches and schools can work together well, it should greatly benefit both. The church can learn how RE is taught in schools and improve on ways to communicate with teenagers. If the minister or visiting Christian speaker is seen as a genuine person, it can challenge false stereotypes and the church can be seen as a relevant community of believers interested in a wide range of contemporary issues. The school can also benefit by using the speaker's experience of teaching about Jesus and other related Christian topics. There is also the opportunity for students to ask questions on their own territory, as some churches can be rather daunting. On a practical level this type of working together is also looked on favourably by OFSTED.

Hopefully everyone will be able to find some useful illustrations in this collection, as well as some interesting food for thought in this introductory section. At the back of this book I have included an Index of Themes as well as a Scripture Index, which may be helpful to those of you planning an extended programme of assemblies. My aim has been to make the assemblies as fun and innovative as possible, while also making them 'hands on' by using volunteers from the audience as much as possible.

I am very grateful to the many people who have shared their skills and experiences with me as I've put this collection together. I hope you enjoy using them and manage to create some really great assemblies.

THE PLANNING STAGE

THE PRACTICALITIES

There's nothing worse than turning up to do an assembly when nobody really has a clue what's happening. Maybe the school hasn't clearly identified what it wants from the speaker, or maybe the speaker hasn't made their needs clear to the school. With just a small amount of communication you can avoid the nightmare of last-minute dashing around, trying to find OHPs or flip charts, or, even worse, a speaker giving a 20-minute sermon when the school was expecting a short four-minute thought!

SCHOOLS' RESPONSIBILITIES TO SPEAKERS

If you are a teacher, it is advisable to send a letter to visiting speakers highlighting what you expect of them in the way of time and content. Things you should include in such a letter are:

- theme of assembly
- timings—when to arrive, how long to speak, time expected to leave, etc.
- numbers of students, with breakdown of age, gender, faith
- availability of facilities and equipment
- name of contact person to meet on the morning

Of course, once a relationship has been established a phone call will be sufficient, but something a bit more official and organised is a good starting-point.

SPEAKERS' RESPONSIBILITIES TO SCHOOLS

Before the day make sure you know all you need to about the time and content of your slot. If you need the school to provide any equipment, organise this well in advance and not on the morning you arrive. I also like to know the name of the teacher I will be meeting at reception. (Unless you arrange this, with the busy nature of the teaching profession it is very easy for the job to fall between two posts.) Lastly, stick to time! However good your assembly is, you can easily outstay your welcome, as most teachers (if not the pupils) will resent losing precious minutes from their next class.

Some of these points may seem rather obvious, but to have a simple checklist ensuring the basics are covered frees you to concentrate on the content.

THE NITTY-GRITTY!
Although getting the practicalities sorted is important when working together with a school, the relationship will inevitably sink or swim on the content of what you say in the assembly. If the school has asked for something on Third World poverty and you give a ten-minute sermon on the sacrificial qualities of the blood of the Lamb, it's likely you won't be invited back, even if you did turn up on time!

The key is simple: we go in as servants to the school, so we give them what they want, and not what we think they need. This isn't to say we're a doormat. If the school asks us to speak on a topic we are unhappy about, we're at perfect liberty to decline their invitation. Often the schools give a speaker a choice of theme, which is great, but we may first have to earn our stripes. The more we are able to prove we can effectively supply a need when it is given, the more flexibility we'll probably be granted in the future.

Each of the illustrations in this collection provides the framework for a complete assembly, from opening lines to ways to conclude. Although it's all there, ready to use, it's still worth spending some time thinking it through and planning. The outlines are not written as unchangeable scripts, but in the hope that individuals will use their own style and make changes, substituting personal stories and so on.

Here's a quick checklist of questions to answer before you begin.

- Have I got an agreed theme/content?
- Do I know exactly how long it should last?
- Do I know the approximate number and age of the students?
- Have I informed the school of any equipment I need?
- Do I know what time to arrive and who to meet?
- Have I got any necessary props?
- Have I adequately prepared/rehearsed the assembly?
- Have I avoided the use of Christian jargon?

WHAT CAN I REALISTICALLY ACHIEVE?

This is a question that stops a lot of people getting involved in this type of work and goes back to our original poser, 'What's the point of doing an assembly?' If you're expecting to do an assembly and see dozens of kids run to the front, falling on their knees in repentance, you might be a bit disappointed. However, there is much you can achieve by posing questions and encouraging personal enquiry.

IN A SENTENCE

One good pointer, and certainly something I like to use, is to sum up in a single sentence what you're basically trying to communicate. Obviously there is only so much you can say in a short assembly slot, so it's good to have clearly in mind the central point you're trying to make. In other words, don't worry about all the things you're not saying or are skipping over, but focus on what you do want to say.

REMEMBER YOU'RE NOT THERE TO PREACH

Some Christian speakers feel that unless they give a full gospel message every single time they speak, they are in some way failing in their duty. I couldn't disagree more. Of course I believe in boldly preaching the gospel, and I love doing it, but there is a time and a place.

I believe we need to exercise great sensitivity to what is essentially a captive audience of pupils (and staff). On the other hand, we mustn't be scared of mentioning God and should feel free to do our job of explaining more about the Christian faith.

When presenting a Christian viewpoint, do so in such a way that someone with a different viewpoint cannot take offence. For instance, use phrases such as 'Christians believe' or 'as a Christian I believe'. You should also avoid using simplistic statements that can make it sound as though belief in Jesus will make everything rosy in the garden. I've spoken to teachers who aren't Christians who feel hypocritical speaking about the Christian faith. As a Christian you are not being asked to actively promote something you don't believe in. However, by using the ambiguous phrases I've mentioned, you're simply stating what Christians believe rather than your own personal opinion.

In this collection a wide range of issues is covered, including drugs, bullying and poverty. This form of assembly is an act of law rather than an act of evangelism. Yes, take the opportunity to make some challenging observations, but release yourself from the pressure of being the second Billy Graham.

POSE QUESTIONS NOT ANSWERS

It is extremely effective to pose provoking questions that demand thought on the part of the individual. If you give people simple answers, all wrapped up in a pretty pink bow, they'll quickly forget what you said and probably think you rather arrogant. But if you leave them with a teaser, some at least will think about it afterwards.

For instance, if talking about life and death it's easy to give the basic Christian response, without allowing people time to think it through for themselves. However, if you add some questions, 'But what do you think? Do you agree or disagree? Why?', you are demanding personal thought and enquiry. Of course some people will have forgotten all you just said, but you can also guarantee that some will continue the questioning in their minds . . . maybe only until break time, maybe until lunchtime, but maybe longer . . .

TAKING CONTROL

The mere thought of standing up in front of 600 teenagers whose expressions range from disinterest to hostility is another reason people choose not to do assemblies. Let's be honest: standing up there all on your own is probably the best laxative known to man! Once you can get over the initial fear, though, your task will be made a lot easier if you can take control from the beginning and cause the students to sit up in their seats and pay attention.

But how can you take control and retain your image of being a reasonably nice person rather than an oppressive dictator? Well, strange as it may seem, my number one piece of advice is don't try to be cool! Believe me, if you do, it just won't work. I've seen people go into school trying to be cool and trendy, wearing the latest clothes and trainers, but basically the kids think they're idiots. You've simply got to take a risk and be yourself. Go in with an attitude of not being over-sensitive about being the brunt of a joke. At core you need to come across as a genuine and sincere person. Within the short confines of an assembly, you need to get their attention quickly. With no more than ten minutes, there's no time for a subtle build up—you've got to grab them quickly and not let go. There's a variety of ways to do this, but here are a few ideas:

- Be quick! Teenagers are used to quick-fire forms of communication. Their attention span is not very long.
- Be visual! Don't just stand there rambling on. Move around, use overheads, video clips, illustrations, etc.
- Be funny! Obviously this is more natural for some than for others and you need to be comfortable with it. Hopefully some of the illustrations in this collection will be amusing.
- Be clear! Have an objective you want to achieve and stick to it rather than wandering all around the houses.
- Be relevant! When using examples, make sure they are relevant to the age group. With a music illustration be aware that the kids may never have heard of Take That and you can be sure they've never heard of Roxy Music!
- Be friendly! I'm a huge advocate of audience participation. By getting the familiar faces of peers on the stage, your listeners will become more interested and involved. (Note: This can be more effective when planned in advance with the school, who will know who *not* to invite up on stage.)

These are just a few pointers, but ultimately the skill of communication is in how you sell what you are saying. If you are apathetic, the assembly will die a slow death. However, if you're enthusiastic, without seeming like a children's presenter on a caffeine overload, your energy will be infectious.

This little section has mainly been about methods of communication, but it is worth saying that for truly successful communication we need two key elements:

1. Something good to say.
2. An effective way of saying it.

If you've got the most amazing, life-changing piece of information but put it over in a drab and boring way so that no one listens, you haven't succeeded. On the other hand, if you have the most brilliant, original, funny and visual way of communicating but have nothing that's really worth saying, again it's all pretty pointless. Have an objective, a clear picture of what you want to say, and in your own style make it as interesting as possible for the listener. Then you will see positive results.

THE CLEVERLY-WORDED LINK

I don't know about you, but I've always cringed at those Radio 4 'Thought for the Day' style presentations where the vicar regales an amusing tale about fixing a pipe, walking the dog or painting a ceiling, only to link it with those immortal words, 'and that's a little bit like Jesus, isn't it?' Perhaps I'm being over-critical, but to be honest I wince every time. I heard one recently where Jesus resembled a boomerang for some surreal reason. As clumsy as these links are, though, there is a lesson in there about a very valuable mode of communication—the art of the tenuous link.

Jesus has probably been compared to every household item imaginable, and while I'm not suggesting we start telling the school children of the United Kingdom that he is a bit like a Breville sandwich toaster, I would advocate linking an illustration into a chosen piece of teaching.

As I mentioned in the last section, it's not enough just to have something relevant to say; we need to engage an audience first so they will actually listen to us. This is where effective and fun illustrations can be so useful. Once we understand that the illustration is there purely to serve as an attention grabber, we will give ourselves the freedom to use these links for a wide range of teaching.

I used to work with a group of people doing talks, sketches and illustrations in a variety of settings. We would challenge one another to work out a good link between one of our pieces and any given theme. For instance, how can you link an illustration where you crack eggs over the heads of volunteers to teaching on the Trinity? (An egg is three in one, of course!) The point is simple: just because an illustration is traditionally linked with one specific teaching doesn't mean that with a bit of clever thinking it can't be linked to something different.

I hope that as you read the plans in this book you won't find the various links I've used too clumsy. Also, if you see an illustration you really want to use but it's linked with a teaching that is not appropriate, be creative! Think of another way to link the chosen illustration to the theme you have to speak on.

USING HUMOUR

There can be no doubt that using humour in assemblies is an absolute winner, as it is in most situations. People love to laugh, and if they are laughing they are generally engaged and absorbed in what you are saying. It is worth bearing in mind, though, the cruel reality that some people simply are funnier than others. Some can effortlessly create wild gales of laughter with anything they do or utter, whereas others can sweat blood and tears working on a gag only to be greeted by a cruel, steely silence. You need to be honest about where on this sliding scale you come in. If using humour just isn't your thing, don't try to push it. Stay real and by all means use amusing stories and illustrations, but don't worry if it doesn't result in people curled up with hysteria. If you find humour a successful tool for you, use it wisely, ensuring things don't go totally over the top at the expense of the message being lost within the delivery.

Here are a few hints on using humour during a presentation.

Be prepared to look silly
If you can, use funny personal stories to illustrate points. People warm to a speaker who is happy to be the brunt of a joke.

Use good props
Depending on the illustration, some well thought out amusing props always go down well. Even if you think you're not particularly good at comedy, you can't fail with a bag of inanimate objects!

Be messy
Obviously check this out with the school in advance, but getting in a bit of a mess is usually good fun. Don't let things descend into pathetic farce, but a cracked egg, spilt water or a broken plate (used wisely) will grab attention.

Use volunteers
This for me is an important key to a good assembly. If you involve people, the group will pay more attention. Of course you introduce the risk of an unknown element, so good planning is imperative. There is a skill to selecting a good

volunteer, and I admit I sometimes pick the worst possible person! Basically you don't want someone so shy they can't speak, but neither do you want the cockiest big mouth in the school! As mentioned earlier, you can always ask for the help of a teacher you trust when making a selection.

Be kind

It is always a temptation to use quite cynical and sarcastic humour, because it's cruel and gets more laughs. However, this comes at a cost and in most instances should be avoided. It is fine to have some fun banter with volunteers, but don't in any way put them down or make them into a laughing-stock. This should also extend to the school as a whole. You may get a laugh if you have a gibe at a particular teacher or the lumpy custard in the school canteen, but it's very bad form and will very likely come back in your face (particularly the custard!). Basically, don't go there!

BUILDING LINKS WITH A SCHOOL

For most people using this book, I imagine there is already a link into a particular school and an opportunity to run assemblies and maybe even lunchtime clubs and lessons. If, however, you are not currently linked with a school there are basically two routes to setting up a partnership.

THROUGH PERSONAL CONTACT

This is how most relationships between schools and churches begin. A teacher, parent or member of the ancillary staff is linked to your church, and they are in a position to approach the school's headteacher or head of religious studies. From here you can work out the needs of the school, and the services you would be able to provide. If there is a contact in the school who can vouch for you or your organisation, this will go down better than coming in cold.

THROUGH COLD CONTACT

Although this is trickier, as you're basically starting from scratch, it is certainly not outside the realms of possibility. While at university, a friend of mine set up a Christian theatre company with some friends and they performed sketches and various talks and illustrations. They contacted some local schools, one of which was very keen to set up a meeting. The result was a greatly successful relationship between the school and the group, which continues now, albeit with new personnel.

Some schools may be uncomfortable with the idea of one particular Christian denomination coming into the school. If this is a problem in your situation, is there any way you could go forward in partnership with another church or group of churches? This would also have the added advantage of pooling the resources different churches may possess. Alternatively, maybe you could go in under the banner of a Christian organisation that doesn't have a specific denominational slant. I used to work with a Third World mission agency and schools opened their arms to us because of the interesting link between the spiritual and cultural elements. I also know of a Christian sailing centre that has a great schools ministry and a very positive reputation among staff and pupils alike.

It's difficult to write in detail how you can build a link with a school, as no two relationships will be totally alike. I believe that as long as you seek to serve in what you do, and bear in mind the DfEE directive quoted earlier, you should gain a positive reputation at the school. Once this has happened, perhaps things can develop beyond simply doing assemblies into running other clubs, lessons and maybe even arranging a school visit to your church.

These brief opening chapters are in no way meant to be exhaustive, but I hope they give you some great ideas to plan and run successful assemblies, helping you further with whatever work you are involved in.

SYMBOLS USED

To help you identify suitable material for your assembly as quickly as possible we have used a series of symbols as a guide to the content and recommended target age range of each assembly.

TARGET AGE RANGE
Because individual pupils, year groups and schools can differ quite considerably, we have labelled the assemblies by Key Stage rather than specific year groups.

KS1 KS2 KS3 KS4

The main Key Stages will appear in bold print while Key Stages for which the assembly could be adapted are in a grey font.

KS2 KS3 KS4

Where a Key Stage symbol is in grey it should be assumed that the assembly would most suit the end of the Key Stage nearest to the Key Stages in bold print. Thus the example above would indicate that pupils in Years 5 and 6 might find the assembly helpful but Years 3 and 4 less so. Equally the example below would indicate that you could possibly use the assembly with Year 10 but less likely with Year 11.

Where an assembly is shown as being suitable for a wide age range, the assumption is that the style of presentation, the tone of voice and vocabulary will be adjusted accordingly. While these outlines are basically 'off the peg' assemblies, some thought must be given to *how* they will be presented.

CONTENT OF MATERIAL

 Requires willing volunteers. Although most of the outlines are for interactive assemblies, these require volunteers to join you on stage.

 Controversial. These assemblies may prove controversial, either in content or format. It is well to check with your contact in the school prior to using them.

 Slightly whacky. These are really fun ideas, but there is a fine line to tread before going 'over the top', so be careful in your preparation.

 Drama. These assemblies are dramas enacted by you and/or your colleagues and require rehearsal in advance.

 Overtly Christian. All the assemblies have some spiritual point but these ones are overtly Christian.

 Crowd control. These assemblies involve some form of active audience participation. This works easier in smaller assemblies. In larger assemblies it can be harder to settle the pupils and regain control so modification may be needed.

PART ONE

PERSONAL, SOCIAL AND MORAL DEVELOPMENT

AN UNLIKELY TRUTH

THEMES: Choices, decision-making process, peer pressure.

INTRODUCTION: This is a simple and effective illustration of the human decision-making process and how we make our choices. While planning you will need to rack your brains and think of a fact about your life that is a bit strange, unlikely or, better still, totally unbelievable. The illustration will sink or swim on the unlikely nature of the truth!

OUTLINE: Open the assembly by explaining that it is necessary for everybody to stand up at a particular point. Rehearse by all standing up, then sitting down again. Comment on how impressed you are by everyone's energy! (If you prefer, the exercise works just as well with putting hands up.)

Now explain that you are going to run a competition and the rules are very simple. You will give them three facts about your life, all of which seem untrue, but one is totally true. The aim is obviously to select the right one. Also say that tempting as it is to copy others or discuss the answer, it is better to go for what you think and have the courage of your convictions.

Now give them an a,b,c choice of facts, putting one true in among two false. As I said in the introduction, the more obscure the better. Throw a few ideas around and I'm sure you'll come up with some classics. Some of the true ones I or my colleagues have used are enjoying a glass of champagne with an Oscar-winning actor, playing cricket at Lord's, and appearing as a policeman in the last episode of *Inspector Morse*. Some of the lies I've used have varied from being a world darts championship finalist, writing a best-selling book and being related to Alan Shearer!

Give the assembly a few seconds to decide, then one at a time repeat the options, asking them to stand for the one they believe to be true. (If at this stage it is noticeable that people are copying their neighbours, it is good to comment on this in a light-hearted way, pointing out how important it is not to just go with the crowd but to make up our own mind.)

Before you give the answer, court some responses to these two questions: 1. What prompted you to make your particular choice? 2. Given more time, how would you have tried to make a more accurate choice? Answers should include fact-finding responses such as checking the Internet, asking people, phoning a darts organisation or even Alan Shearer! In other words, to make educated choices we need to be informed first.

Reveal the answer and get the winners to stand for a round of applause. Link into how we make choices—that they should be our own and they should be thought through and researched—and that they can have lasting consequences.

TEACHING POINT: Be informed before you make any decisions.

BIBLE REFERENCE: Proverbs 18:13.

APPLICATION: Can be easily adapted for use in any situation, and gives scope for making a point about deciding to follow Christ.

THE GREAT EGG CHALLENGE

THEMES: Choices, consequences.

INTRODUCTION: I guarantee that this very easy to prepare illustration will have even the most hardened and sceptical customers eating out of your hands! I've used it countless times with the dependable effect of bored assembly fodder turning into a highly excitable crowd.

The basic point is that in life we have choices and those choices have consequences, some big and some not so big. The challenge for your volunteers is to choose the egg that will lead to the positive consequence of a prize, not the negative consequence of egg quite literally all over their faces! Great fun and very easy to lead into a thought-provoking message.

YOU WILL NEED
- four eggs: three hard-boiled and one raw
- a damp cloth
- three dustbin liners opened at the seams to create a large sheet
- three chocolate bars

OUTLINE: As an introduction, relay a story about how often in life we make choices. Personalise some choices you made this morning—what to eat for breakfast, what to wear, whether to feed the dog, etc. . . . anything light-hearted will serve the purpose.

Go on to explain how the choices we make inevitably have consequences. Some not as major as others, but consequences nonetheless. Use examples again, such as romantic partners, where to live, which options to choose . . .

Now say that to illustrate this point you have a challenge. If anyone is brave enough to take up this challenge and make the right choice, they will win a chocolate bar! (At this point try to encourage some participatory whoops and cheers!) However, if they make the wrong choice they will get egg on their face.

Next show them the four eggs, explaining that one is raw and the other three are hard-boiled. Explain the rules of the challenge, that a volunteer will be selected to come on stage, sit on a chair and choose an egg. That egg will then be smashed on their head! If it is hard-boiled, they win and receive chocolate. If it is raw, they will look incredibly silly and win nothing. (By this point there should be some excited murmurs and probably a few volunteer hands.)

Choose your volunteer and make a big drama about sitting them down and wrapping the bin liner around them like an apron in a barber shop. When they choose the egg, again milk the audience for reaction and opinion. Use classic lines such as 'Final answer?' or 'Do you want to phone a friend?'

After a loud group countdown, crack the egg on the volunteer's head, checking they are well covered if it is the raw one. Award a prize if it is hard-boiled.

The illustration can last as long as you have the raw egg and willing volunteers. (The latter should never be a problem.) Each time warn the volunteer of the worsening odds, indicating the importance of bearing this in mind when we make choices in life.

This may seem a bit sneaky, but if possible leave the raw egg till last, carefully switching it if it's chosen earlier. If the raw egg is last, it leads to a lovely comic moment where you can challenge a volunteer to call your bluff, as by this stage the audience will be thinking that all the eggs are hard-boiled. The volunteer will of course find out in the stickiest way that you were not bluffing! (This is the reason for keeping the damp cloth handy.)

From this exercise you have an engaged audience, and a platform to give your chosen message. Depending on the situation, you can vary this to any suitable topic, including choices regarding religion, friends, drugs, options . . . The list is endless.

On a practical note, make sure to keep the volunteer well protected to minimise the mess; and when cracking the hard-boiled egg, take it easy—if you do it very hard it will really hurt! Check with the head teacher responsible before using this idea. Use eggs guaranteed free from salmonella.

TEACHING POINT: Personal responsibility for the choices we make.

BIBLE REFERENCES: Genesis 2:15–17; Romans 1:24–32.

APPLICATION: The flexible nature of this illustration makes it suitable for many different topics by simply tweaking your message at the end.

ULTIMATE MULTIPLE CHOICE

KS2 KS3 KS4

THEMES: Choices, Jesus.

INTRODUCTION: I've always loved that famous C. S. Lewis quote in which he reduces all the different arguments about who Jesus is into a very simple choice of three options: liar, lunatic or Lord. After opening this assembly with a multiple choice quiz on any topic, you can work towards this challenge, which is as effective now as the day it was first penned.

YOU WILL NEED
• OHP and prepared acetates

OUTLINE: Open the assembly by asking who enjoys exams. Perhaps relate a short story of your time as an exam-taking pupil, ending with the thought that multiple choice papers were your favourite, as they at least gave you the chance of having a last ditch stab in the dark!

Announce that you will now be running a short multiple choice quiz. I would suggest that no more than three questions are needed. Make up your own questions based on what's of current interest—who's number 1 in the charts, who won the football league, anything about soaps, films, major news events, etc.

You can run the quiz in one of two ways: either ask for volunteers (perhaps two teams of two) or do it as a whole assembly exercise, asking people to stand for the option they believe is correct. For each question, put the options up on an acetate, preferably with some pictures.

After giving the answers, say that for each question there was obviously only one correct answer, but if someone chose incorrectly, it was understandable as it was offered as an option. For instance, if offered the options Paris, London or New York to the question 'What is the capital of France?' London is obviously the wrong answer but it was at least an option. It would not be possible to answer Oslo, as it wasn't even an offered option.

With this in mind, now show one more question, asking the assembly not to answer out loud but just consider whether Jesus Christ was (a) a liar, (b) a lunatic or (c) Lord. Unpack each statement, saying that Jesus claimed he was the Son of God but he could have been purposely lying, he could have been barking mad or he could have been telling the truth. Further explain that many see Jesus as just a good man or some form of moral teacher, but logic dictates this is not an option. Jesus is either exactly who he says he is, or else he is mad or a liar. Because of his wild claims, just a nice guy is one thing he cannot be, and as C. S. Lewis (who wrote the Narnia stories) put it, it was never an option he intended to leave us.

TEACHING POINT: That Jesus must be the Son of God.

BIBLE REFERENCE: Luke 9:18–20.

APPLICATION: A thought-provoking challenge on who the assembly thinks Jesus really is.

CAT FOOD CUISINE

 KS2 KS3  KS4

THEMES: Appearances, misconceptions.

INTRODUCTION: Here's a good one to get a few stomachs churning in an early morning assembly! It takes a bit of preparation beforehand, but it's worth the effort for the reaction you get as you pick up a can-opener, open a tin of cat food, then stick in a spoon and eat a mouthful! I've done this before to screeches of disgust, but it really grabs the attention. Of course you don't have to actually eat cat food—in fact what you eat tastes pretty good, and you have a perfect link to how appearances can be deceptive.

YOU WILL NEED
- cat food label
- empty tin (not from cat food)
- orange jelly mix
- Snickers bar
- can-opener
- prize

OUTLINE: The day before, you will need to prepare your fake tin of cat food. Simply take an empty tin and pour in an orange jelly mix to a quarter full. Chop a Snickers bar into slices and drop half in. When set, fill up the tin with more jelly mix and drop in the rest of the Snickers. (The reason for staggering is to get the most density of chocolate at the bottom of the tin, which for the illustration will actually be the top of the tin.)

Put in the fridge overnight. Now put the tin lid back on, holding it securely in place with Sellotape. Finally, stick the cat food label on upside down, so the unopened bottom becomes the top.

Open the assembly by telling the story of an old lady who had mistakenly been buying cat food and eating it herself for months. Embellish some details to try and get a revolted response. Go on to say that however disgusting it sounds it would be worth trying it out just to see. At this point get out the tin of cat food and start to open the tin. (Once open you will see how the mix of jelly and Snickers has a deceptive cat food appearance!) If you are near enough to pupils, show the tin around.

Very cautiously sniff the cat food and recoil, furthering the pupils' misconception about the content. Next dip in your little finger and lick it. This will be greeted with groans. Then get a spoon and eat a big mouthful—this could potentially get squeals!

Now ask for a volunteer. You may think it's impossible that anyone would volunteer, but although some will be disgusted and fooled, many will realise it's not really cat food. If you do get a volunteer, let them take a mouthful, elicit some applause and give them a prize.

Tell the assembly what was contained in the tin and explain how you tricked them. Link this to the fact that often we allow appearances to pepper our view of things, but they can be deceptive. We so easily allow other people or the media to guide our thoughts, and this can often lead to huge misunderstanding.

Further link this to how people perceive Christians, and how so often this is far removed from the reality of what Christ stands for.

TEACHING POINT: Appearances can be deceptive.

BIBLE REFERENCE: 1 Samuel 16:7.

APPLICATION: Although you could make this more general, it works best linked with misconceptions about Christianity.

THIRST QUENCHER

THEMES: Masks, inner self versus outward appearance.

INTRODUCTION: This is another simple illustration that needs a minimal amount of preparation. Having worked your assembly up into a sweat, you offer to quench their thirst by squirting a can of fizzy drink all over them! Although you don't actually do it, the illustration works particularly well if you have previously done 'The Great Egg Challenge' (Idea 1), ensuring the assembly will be in no doubt that you are prepared to make a mess!

The themes you can link into can be a more moral approach on how our outward appearance doesn't always reflect what's inside, or the Christian message on how we have an emptiness in ourselves without God.

YOU WILL NEED
- a can of fizzy drink
- a screwdriver

OUTLINE: Before the assembly begins you will need to doctor a can of fizzy drink. Simply make a little hole by the ridge on the bottom of the can, and then drain out all the drink, making sure there are no drops left. (A visible drip will spoil the effect.)

At the opening, announce how hard you find it to conduct assemblies when everybody is half-asleep. (Pick on a few people here if you feel brave.) Then say, 'To get us going we are going to do a wake-up exercise.'

Lead any form of loud, physical exercise, be it keep-fit stretches, an audience participation rhyme or some form of wild movement. Anything will suffice, but be as creative as possible taking into account the limitations of space and numbers.

As you invite people to sit back down, tell them how tired and thirsty you are and that you could do with some refreshment. Of course you would love to share it with them, but unfortunately you only have one can of drink.

At this point, fake a moment of inspiration. Position a chair for you to stand on, front and centre, and announce that you have a great sharing idea. Stand on the chair and start shaking the can violently. (This should worry the people in the front rows.) Ask everyone to tilt their heads back and open their mouths. There will be an obvious reluctance to obey this command, but get as many people to join in as possible.

At the crescendo of expectation, crack open the can. Obviously nothing will happen, so pull off the tab and tip the can upside down, showing it's empty. This will get some disappointed groans (except from the first rows).

Explain how annoying it is that the drink looked so enticing from the outside (cool and refreshing and thirst-quenching), but on the inside it was empty and incapable of delivering its promise.

Link this into your chosen theme, saying how we often put on an outward show, promising much, but failing to live up to it. Politicians make all sorts of promises, then often fail to deliver when in power. Pop stars tell their fans to live wholesome lives, then get caught in sex and drug scandals. Maybe a friend appears to be loyal, then lets us down in the worst possible way. How important it is that we strive to be consistent, truthfully delivering on our outward promises.

For a Christian message, further link by explaining the Christian belief that Jesus is the ultimate example of fulfilling a promise. He does exactly what it says on the tin. He removes the feeling of emptiness we can have on the inside and gives our life purpose through a living relationship with God.

TEACHING POINT: Is our outward appearance an honest reflection of how we feel inside?

BIBLE REFERENCE: Proverbs 19:22.

APPLICATION: This can be employed simply as a lesson on personal development, or further expanded to explain the basics of Christianity.

CALL MY BLUFF

THEMES: Deception, wisdom.

INTRODUCTION: Life brings us many choices, and included in this book are suggestions for assemblies based on that topic. However, we are sometimes dealt cards from a rigged deck. Choices are made more difficult by people not being totally honest; trying to deceive us into buying something, signing something or voting for something. We need to be sure we are not being duped and always be aware that the wolves come in sheep's clothing.

Using the famous panel game *Call My Bluff* as an illustration, you can easily link into teaching on this important lesson.

YOU WILL NEED
- overhead with *Call My Bluff* questions
- prize

OUTLINE: Begin by telling the assembly a story about you or someone you know having been duped. It can be true, completely made up or lifted from a newspaper. You can use something general like a political party (without mentioning a particular one) promising to do something if you vote them in, only to renege on their promise once they are in power. You can be more light-hearted, with something like the example of booking into a luxury villa, only to arrive at a half-finished building site! Alternatively, go for something typical, like the aggressive techniques used by some salesmen to get a signature on the dotted line. Your basic thrust is that unfortunately in life some people make a career from lying, deceiving, duping and bluffing.

Next introduce the game *Call My Bluff*. Select some volunteers, perhaps two boys against two girls for a battle of the sexes. Obviously in the panel game each team tries to bluff the other. Alternatively, if you're a bit pressed for time, you can pose the questions yourself, asking each team in turn for a response. Here are a couple of suggestions I got from my dictionary (asterisk denotes correct definition), but I'm sure you'll have no problem finding your own.

Cankerworm
(a) Larva of a moth.*
(b) An Australian pesticide.
(c) An old English word to describe a miserable person.

Nudicaudate
(a) An animal with a hairless tail.*
(b) A dating agency for naturists.
(c) A collective syndicate of companies.

Having completed the competition, encourage some applause and award a prize.

Link into the fact that making choices is hard enough, without people purposely trying to put obstacles in the way to fool or bluff us. We need to make sure we are informed and careful about what and who we put our trust in.

You can now further link this to the Bible's teaching on wolves in sheep's clothing. Christians believe that people will come trying to deceive, offering tantalising alternatives to a life of true faith. They will offer easy, tempting options, but the Christian is warned to follow only the teaching of Jesus, however attractive alternatives may appear.

TEACHING POINT: Be careful of what and whom you trust.

BIBLE REFERENCE: Matthew 7:15.

APPLICATION: Depending on the depth of link into biblical teaching, you can talk about Jesus being the way, the *truth* and the life.

TELLING TALES

KS2   KS3   KS4

THEMES: Deception, truth, appearances and choices.

INTRODUCTION: On my local radio station they play a quiz most mornings, where three presenters all tell a story and it is down to the listener to vote for which of the three they believe to be telling the truth.

Using this basic but very engaging framework, you will need to co-opt three colleagues or friends to assist you in giving this fun illustration on deception, truth and not judging a book by its cover. Where you have a good relationship with the school, this could be done with three members of staff whom the pupils think they know well! Before the assembly, decide on a theme for the stories you are going to tell. It could be 'The day I met . . .', 'I used to be a . . .' and so on.

YOU WILL NEED
• three other presenters

OUTLINE: Open the assembly by saying that this morning you are going to have a bit of a well-deserved rest and leave all the hard work to some friends you've brought in, and later on the whole assembly!

One by one introduce the three guests, exaggerating their positive traits and upright character, trustworthiness and general goodness! However, two are about to lie! Explain that each of the three will tell a short and exciting story about themselves on the chosen theme. (Obviously to a certain degree the assembly will sink or swim on how good these stories are and how well they are told, so choose your assistants wisely.)

Once told, briefly summarise the stories and elicit some response from the assembly as to how confident they are about knowing the true one. Take a standing vote to find who is the winner and most believed.

Next, ask a few people to explain why they chose the person they did. Reasons may include: looked honest, sounded feasible, other stories seemed far-fetched, story was told well or sold effectively. (The reality, of course, is that many just go along with what their friends do!) Ceremoniously reveal the identity of the true storyteller and congratulate the winners.

Link this to the point of how easy it is to be deceived or taken in by someone masquerading as something they are not. We are warned from childhood (and rightly so) of being wary of strangers, yet many are used and abused by those hidden in their close circle of family and friends. We are tempted into smoking by advertisements using good-looking models to blind us to the harmful effects on our health. Silver-tongued salesmen can con us into buying something we don't want and they can't deliver.

TEACHING POINT: Do not allow yourselves to be deceived.

BIBLE REFERENCE: Colossians 2:8.

APPLICATION: Christians believe that people can be spiritually deceived. So many things look good and tempt us away from the truth of God's word. In all things we must be discerning so that in no areas of our lives do we fall prey to falsehood.

A ROMANTIC MEAL FOR TWO

THEMES: Contracts, deception, discernment, small print.

INTRODUCTION: We all know that offering teenagers a prize of chocolate has always been a huge incentive to encourage active involvement, but how about offering them something a bit more substantial—say, a romantic meal for two anywhere in your local area? By setting up a competition between a couple of students you can get the whole assembly focused on the big prize, but then they find out about the small print.

Making the point about being conned and checking contracts, the teaching can also be linked to the no-hidden-catch message of the gospel. This assembly could be particularly effective around Valentine's Day.

YOU WILL NEED
- props for your chosen competition
- a pot noodle with two plastic forks

OUTLINE: Open by explaining that due to the generosity of the school budget, this morning during assembly you have a really fantastic prize to award one lucky student. Really build this up so that everyone is intrigued. Announce that the prize is a romantic meal for two anywhere in your local area! Encourage a few excited whoops and cheers.

Now choose some volunteers to contend for the prize. The competition you choose can be anything ranging from a quiz to some kind of physical or sports challenge. My personal favourite involves selecting two guys, and then presenting both with a large pair of old-fashioned Y-fronts! They have to put these on over their trousers, which in itself gets a big laugh, then they have to pull them right down to their ankles, then back up again as many times as possible within 60 seconds. It's quite fun also to pick a couple of girls to act as judges, counting the results. Of course, during this game go overboard getting the rest of the pupils to cheer and encourage the chosen guys to go faster!

This game always gets a great reaction, but if you feel it's not suitable, absolutely any contest will suffice.

Announce your winner and present them with the prize—a pot noodle with two forks! (A romantic meal for two anywhere in your local area . . . get it?) There may be a few complaints and jeers, but of course you're covered—the prize accurately fits its earlier description.

Link this to how we need to be aware of what we sign up for: contracts with crippling small print; agreements that bind us to a particular product for life; debt plans that just sink us further into debt. Unfortunately many people are dishonest, and will try to persuade you to sign your life away.

Further link this to the fact that people often believe that Christianity asks you to sign your life away, making you into a weird, chanting, sandal-wearing geek— all of which is untrue. (Though the sandals are obviously an option!)

TEACHING POINT: The Bible has no hidden catches or clauses.

BIBLE REFERENCE: Isaiah 59:21.

APPLICATION: Christians believe that the Bible has no hidden catches: it is clear in what it offers and expects of an individual. Yes, we must commit our lives to Christ, following his teaching, but our commitment to him is far outstripped by his commitment to us—past, present and future.

SOCK IN A TEAPOT

THEMES: Deception, appearances.

INTRODUCTION: Here's a good illustration that pretty much guarantees a positive audience response, giving you the opportunity to link into a range of messages.

The basic idea is the classic 70s cola challenge (Pepsi, Coke or Panda pops), slightly altered so it is poured from a teapot! It is easy to link into teaching on the deceptive qualities of outward appearances.

YOU WILL NEED
- a teapot
- a sock
- various brands of cola

OUTLINE: Open the assembly by running a quick poll on what people drink in the morning before school. Coffee, tea, water, soft drink, something else? Encourage some responses and add a few comments such as: 'I personally believe you shouldn't trust anyone who doesn't start the morning with at least two cups of coffee!'

Next, show off your teapot (the flashier the better). Explain that due to there being no electricity on stage, you can't offer anyone a cup of tea, but there is an alternative available. At this point choose a couple of volunteers to join you.

Once you have your volunteers, pour them a drink from the teapot. (It's cola, but at this point they don't know that.) Challenge them to drink it, then ask what they think it is. They will obviously know it's cola, but now move on to the classic challenge, asking them if they think it's Coke, Pepsi or a third, cheap brand. Announce the result, congratulating where appropriate.

Now try and pour yourself a glass, but discover there is none left. This is where your acting abilities come into play. Look into the teapot and feign shock, apologising for a slight problem. You then hook out of the teapot a sock, dripping in cola—the same cola the volunteers have just drunk! For extra comic effect, roll up your trouser leg to reveal a missing sock, saying something like, 'I was looking for that sock for ages this morning because I've only worn it for three days so far!'

Thank the volunteers and get them to sit back down. Perhaps award them with a fresh can of drink to wash away the cheesy aroma!

For your message, link in the basic point that appearances can be deceptive. From the outside, things can look very impressive, but on the inside the story is very different.

TEACHING POINT: Appearances can be deceptive.

BIBLE REFERENCE: Colossians 2:8.

APPLICATION: You can further link this to (1) a more general teaching on ensuring we always check out facts and are not deceived, or (2) a more overt Christian message about the Christian belief that without Christ we may look all right on the outside, but inside we are far from perfect and need to turn to him.

GREEDY PIGS

THEMES: Sharing, teamwork.

INTRODUCTION: It can be very easy, particularly as younger people, to view life as a competition. Who can win? Who's the cleverest? Who's the fastest? In short, who will end up on top? In this competitive atmosphere, the idea of sharing, supporting and working together can slip down (or even off) the agenda. Using this fun illustration, you can make the point that pooling resources often works in your own favour. Note: Where this is on a raised stage, ensure the competitors are nowhere near the edge of the stage!

YOU WILL NEED
- two plates
- two chocolate bars, chopped up
- a length of rope, with cushioning
- pig costumes (optional)

OUTLINE: Announce that today the assembly will take the form of a competition or challenge that requires the sheer brute strength of two volunteers. Choose the volunteers, who should be of the same sex and approximately the same size.

Once you have your volunteers, tell them the game is called 'Greedy Pigs' and give them pig costumes to put on. (This is optional but worth the effort. It only needs to be funny little things like ears, nose and tail.)

Now tie the rope around their waists, one volunteer at either end. For protection it is wise to cushion their waists first to limit the rope digging into their flesh.

Next put a plate of chopped up chocolate at either end of the stage, making sure that at full stretch it is impossible to reach the plates. Explain the very basic aim, which is that both greedy pigs want their dinner, and they have a 90-second time limit in which to eat it. Position the pigs at an equal distance from their plates, pull the rope taut, and with much crowd participation and cheering begin the game.

Usually a tug of war will take place, to the delight of the assembly, and there may or may not be an outright winner in the allotted time. It is possible, however, that your volunteers will suss your point about sharing and working together. In this unlikely event, don't be put off; congratulate them on their wisdom. You can also get them to have the tug of war competition anyway, just for fun.

Assuming the volunteers don't work together, at the end of the game explain how much easier it would have been to co-operate, with one allowing the other to get to their plate, and then the second doing the same, giving them both plenty of time to eat in comfort. Demonstrate this, then let the volunteers sit back down with the remaining chocolate.

Link this to the point that in life we so often want to be competitive and succeed on our own, without any help. But, to coin a phrase, 'no man is an island'.

TEACHING POINT: Life is not just a competition.

BIBLE REFERENCE: Acts 2:42–47.

APPLICATION: Further link this to the Christian belief that it is good to share our talents, material possessions and faith in Christ, to strengthen and encourage one another.

ONE BODY, MANY MOUTHS

THEME: Teamwork.

INTRODUCTION: In 'Greedy Pigs' we used a competition to illustrate some advantages of sharing and teamwork over working on your own. In this linked illustration, instead of setting up a competition, give some volunteers a group challenge so they can see the positive effects of working together. Even in seemingly impossible situations, a team is much more powerful than the sum of its individual parts.

This assembly would work best in smaller groups where it will be easier to see what is happening. An assistant to help with the tying up would be helpful, to speed things up and enable you to maintain eye contact with the audience.

YOU WILL NEED
- rope
- belts
- handcuffs (optional)
- a glass of water
- cloths (to mop up the inevitable spillage)
- prizes

OUTLINE: Open by asking if anyone has ever been in a situation where they were totally stumped, and had no idea how they could possibly proceed. Often at times like this it's our family and friends—those closest to us—who prove themselves indispensable with their help.

Now choose five volunteers. They need to be happy about getting close and friendly with each other to take part in the group challenge.

Once you have your volunteers, explain that you are going to bind them together as part of the challenge, which is simply for all five to drink a mouthful of water. When you bind them together, using whatever you like (ropes, belts, handcuffs, blindfolds, rubber rings!), it is best to have some pre-rehearsed configurations worked out. The basic aim is that they are all comically and awkwardly linked, and will only be able to drink with the help of others.

Allow the challenge to go on until completion, or for a given length of time, or until you feel the joke has run its course. Award some prizes and encourage applause. Link this illustration to how in life we can often achieve so much more if we work in teams. Most businesses hold seminars about effective teamwork and how it can increase the potential of an organisation.

Give some examples of successful teamwork: football teams practising set pieces; scuba divers going down with a 'buddy'; team leadership where different people have different skills; politicians who stick together to bail each other out. Pose the question, 'How are your team skills? Do they need to improve?'

Further link this to the biblical teaching that Christians believe God created us to work together, not to be an island. We need to respect one another's skills and abilities and also recognise that we ourselves have an important role to play.

TEACHING POINT: Each of us has an important role to play in a team.

BIBLE REFERENCE: 1 Corinthians 12:12–31.

APPLICATION: The Bible describes us as a body, and just as it is daft for the eye to say to the hand, 'I don't need you', so it is daft for us to try and do things alone.

THE DISPOSABLE PLATE

THEMES: Environment, resources, responsibility.

INTRODUCTION: It might seem that the world we inhabit is a pretty robust kind of place, quite capable of taking a few knocks, but of course the truth is rather different. The way we currently live our lives, without a care for the future, is taking its toll. Our disposable society leaves its piles of mess, waste and toxic emissions, and the environment pays the high price. This assembly aims to introduce the theme of our responsibility to the planet, looking at what is disposable and at what cannot be fixed once broken.

YOU WILL NEED
- a child's jigsaw
- a Lego set
- paper and Sellotape
- a plate
- glue
- a mallet
- a cloth

OUTLINE: Open the assembly by saying how it has struck you that the more society moves on, the more it seems we live in a disposable or chuck-away age. If anything is a bit old, we just throw it out and get a new one.

Mention some of the following, or choose your own to illustrate the point. If possible, back them up with some kind of visual aid.

- As a nation we work our way through literally millions of carrier bags every year. Years ago we would have owned a sturdy shopping bag to reuse.
- We put nappies in a disposable bag and throw them away, when not so many years ago cotton nappies were washed and reused.
- As the prices have fallen, we even get rid of electrical appliances if they don't fit in with our new colour scheme.
- To top it all, we even have disposable contact lenses!

Call up three or four volunteers to help with a challenge to fix something that you break.

1. Get an easy child's jigsaw, break it up and set the volunteer the task of piecing it back together.
2. Now get a Lego model and break that up for the second volunteer to rebuild.
3. Get a picture, tear it up and give it to the next volunteer with a roll of Sellotape.
4. For the grand finale, get a plate, wrap it in a cloth, and with a huge mallet smash it to smithereens. Tip out the pieces for the fourth volunteer and set them to work with a tube of glue. (Note: Be careful with sharp edges! You could adapt this idea for KS1 and KS2 by substituting a rice-krispies cake for the plate. No glue or Sellotape for KS1.)

Let this run for a couple of minutes, checking on the progress, and then judge the results. The point is that all are at least basically fixable except the plate. Encourage some applause as the volunteers sit back down.

Now link the illustration to our responsibilities to the environment and our natural resources. As we dispose of things, creating waste and causing harmful emissions, we are causing a strain on the environment, particularly the much spoken of ozone layer. We can be naïve, saying it'll all be fine, we can fix it or replace it, but some things, like the plate in our illustration, cannot be fixed.

TEACHING POINT: Are we as individuals actively trying to protect the environment?

BIBLE REFERENCE: Genesis 1:26.

APPLICATION: Link to the biblical teaching that God gave mankind dominion over the earth and animals, but with that charge comes the responsibility of care.

A QUESTION OF THE ENVIRONMENT

THEMES: Environment, recycling, green issues.

INTRODUCTION: In political circles the green lobby is beginning to have a bit more clout, and not a moment too soon. Our selfish modern lifestyles are certainly taking their toll, with green-house gases, holes in the ozone layer, energy wastage, acid rain and the extinction of species. As with most threats like these, the thought doesn't please or thrill us, but on the other hand do we care enough personally to make a difference?

   The aim of this assembly is to provoke some thought on various environmental issues, giving some interesting facts, while enjoying a competitive quiz.

YOU WILL NEED
• acetates or visuals for the quiz

OUTLINE: Open by saying that at election time various topics come to the top of the political agenda, with the different parties fighting for votes. These might typically include tax, health, education, Europe, transport—all obviously important—but one that often takes a bit of a backseat is green or environmental issues. The main reason for this is that it's not seen as such a big vote winner among the electorate at large, either because people don't understand the issues, they see them as problems for the future, or they simply don't care! Explain that you are going to look at some facts and also have a bit of a quiz! Choose some volunteers for the quiz: two teams of two or however you prefer to run it. Note: asterisks below denote correct answers.

FACT: The much spoken of ozone layer is a layer of gas that protects the earth from around 97% of the sun's harmful ultraviolet rays. Bearing this in mind, it might be a good idea to protect it and not pump, squirt and spray damaging gases into it.

FACT: Pure air is 78% nitrogen and 21% oxygen, with the rest made up of smaller gases such as argon.

1. Of all the carbon dioxide we put into the air, what percentage is from road traffic?

(a) 10%
(b) 20%*
(c) 30%

2. Which of these contributes an estimated 100 billion tonnes of methane into the air every year?

(a) Factory fumes
(b) Road and air travel
(c) Cattle breaking wind*

3. In Holland, approximately a third of all journeys are made by bicycle. Around what percentage is that in Britain?

(a) 2%*
(b) 12%
(c) 22%

Some of these things are in our power to change; others are a bit more difficult. One thing we can have a big impact on, though, is household waste and recycling.

4. Roughly how much waste does Britain throw away every year?

    (a) 45 million tonnes
    (b) 450 million tonnes*
    (c) 4,500 million tonnes

FACT: On average over a tonne of waste is thrown away from every household each year.

5. How many pairs of wooden chopsticks are thrown away every day in Japan?

    (a) 2 million
    (b) 8 million
    (c) 16 million*

6. Approximately how much water does a family of four use every week?

    (a) 77 gallons
    (b) 770 gallons*
    (c) 7,700 gallons

FACT: Around a third of this is used to flush the loo.

7. We throw away literally billions of cans each year that are made of aluminium, which can be recycled. What percentage do we actually recycle?

    (a) 5%*
    (b) 15%
    (c) 25%

These are just a few interesting facts gleaned from various books and websites, but you can easily replace them with facts and questions of your own.

    Congratulate the contest winners and close the assembly by saying that there are many ways we can personally take responsibility for protecting the environment. But do we really care enough to do so?

TEACHING POINT: Do you care enough about the state of the environment?

BIBLE REFERENCE: Romans 3:19.

APPLICATION: Link to the biblical teaching that God gave mankind dominion over the earth, but with that charge comes the responsibility of care.

OPPOSITE SIDES OF A COIN

THEMES: Friendships, advice, sex.

INTRODUCTION: To perform this sketch in an assembly, you will
need three strong character performers with the ability to switch
comically from male to female roles.

   Although the sketch touches on the theme of sex, its central
teaching is about how we choose who we listen to, and the qualities
we seek in our closest advisors. The piece should be played in a highly
stylised way and no major movement is required. The three performers
stay seated, delivering their lines directly to the audience, except
where there is dialogue between characters.

YOU WILL NEED
•   three chairs

SCRIPT: ONE: Why is life full of such dilemmas?

TWO: Well, it's all part of life's rich tapestry, isn't it?

ONE: And if it's not one thing . . .

THREE: You can bet your life it's something else.

ONE: The car's cream-crackered.

TWO: My hair looks like I've been dragged backwards through a thorny bush.

THREE: The central heating system's making some dodgy rattling noise.

ONE: Not to mention the complete bane of my life—MEN!

TWO: Blokes.

THREE: Geezers.

ONE: Up to all sorts and full of excuses.

TWO: (*As bloke.*) 'Course I didn't forget your birthday, hun; it just temporarily slipped my mind.

THREE: (*As bloke.*) I would have bought you flowers, babe, but I was right out of dosh.

TWO: (*As bloke.*) I wasn't snogging that other bird—honest. She started to faint so I had to give her mouth-to-mouth resuscitation!

ONE: So I had this guy on the go a while back—Dave was his name.

TWO: Painter and decorator.

THREE: Right cheeky chappie.

TWO: Fantastic body.

THREE: And a real eye for the ladies.

ONE: Anyway, we were out one night, celebrating our two-week anniversary, and he gives me the big speech. You know the one.

TWO: (*As Dave.*) Babes, we've been going steady for ages now, and I think we've reached the point in our relationship where it's time to . . . well, you know, move things on to a higher plateau, in a manner of speaking.

ONE: I knew where he was heading with this, but I let him stumble on a bit longer.

THREE: (*As Dave.*) Do you get my drift, babes? What I mean to say is, we can move things on a notch or two in the physical sense, if you know what I mean. I love you so much and I need to explore other avenues to communicate my love for you in a more meaningful way . . . babes.

ONE: In plain English, Dave!

TWO/THREE: Do you wanna have sex?

ONE: I admit Dave didn't have the romantic quality of a Shakespearean sonnet.

TWO: Romeo, Romeo . . .

THREE: Wherefore art thou Romeo . . .

ONE: But I really fancied him, so I temporarily put him off, subject to a couple of essential girlie chats.

TWO: This is where we come in.

THREE: And it all gets well juicy!

ONE: The only thing is, when you ask for a friend's counsel, on the one hand . . .

TWO: You can get really good advice.

ONE: But on the other hand . . .

THREE: You can get really bad advice.

ONE: Bringing us back to the question: why is life full of such dilemmas?

(ONE *and* TWO *face each other;* THREE *freezes.*)

TWO: What did you say his name was?

ONE: Dave.

TWO: And where did you meet him?

ONE: Cinderella's.

TWO: Ooh, classy joint then!

ONE: Don't joke, this is a serious situation.

TWO: Yeah I know, sorry.

ONE: So what should I do? What would you do?

TWO: Hang on, hang on. One question at a time.

ONE: Well, aren't they the same?

TWO: Look, I know what I would do, but at the end of the day that doesn't matter. The only thing that counts is what you're going to do, isn't it?

ONE: Yeah, I suppose.

TWO: So what are you going to do?

ONE: I don't know!

TWO: Well, how long have you known him?

ONE: Two weeks.

TWO: Two weeks! Not exactly established, is it?

ONE: But he says he loves me.

TWO: Oh *please*! He hardly knows you.

ONE: I've seen him virtually every day.

TWO: So what do you know about him?

ONE: Well, he's a painter, he's 22, he holidays in Ibiza, supports Chelsea and he's into Fatboy Slim.

TWO: But what's he like?

ONE: Well . . . he's nice . . . but I suppose he has got a bit of a reputation.

TWO: Oh yeah?

ONE: But he says it's totally different with me.

TWO: And you believe him?

ONE: Yeah . . . I don't know.

TWO: Look, I don't wanna lecture you, but I know what I'd do, and that's apply the brakes big time. If he really loves you, he won't mind waiting, will he?

ONE: (*To audience*.) Of course, this did sound sensible, but as we all know, every coin has two sides.

(ONE *and* THREE *face;* TWO *freezes*.)

THREE: So how's it all going with old Davey boy?

ONE: Pretty well. We've been going steady for about two weeks.

THREE: Two weeks! Blimey, you're a pair of old-timers.

ONE: Do you think?

THREE: 'Course!

ONE: Dave was suggesting we . . . well you know, move things on a step or two.

THREE: Oh yeah? Randy wotsit.

ONE: What do you think I should do?

THREE: Go for it, you dozy mare. You only live once.

ONE: But do you think it's a bit too soon?

THREE: (*Mimics*) Is it a bit too soon? No! Listen to me, girl. Dave is well lush and if you don't get in there while you've got the chance, some other bit's gonna step in. I'd be there myself if I didn't have two kids to look after on my own! Just go for it! Am I right?

ONE: Maybe.

THREE: Definitely.

(*All face front*.)

ONE: So there's the dilemma.

TWO: Two sides of the story.

THREE: Opposite sides of a coin.

ONE: So who did I listen to, I hear you ask?

TWO: Well . . .

THREE: Yeah, come on. Spill the beans.

ONE: No, I'm not saying. I hate those neat little conclusions, and I don't want people judging me one way or the other. All I'll say is that Dave and me are together no more.

TWO: That means she didn't.

THREE: Stroll on! It means she did!

ONE: It means I'll let you draw your own conclusions. Who would you listen to? Who's wise? Who's foolish? And the moral of this tale? Well, I'll let you decide . . .

TEACHING POINT: When seeking advice, look for a wise and unbiased counsellor.

BIBLE REFERENCE: Proverbs 14:7.

APPLICATION: The central theme is as much related to moral and social development as it is to spiritual.

SMELLY KENNY

THEMES: Bullying, friendship.

INTRODUCTION: Although there are a few laughs at various points in this sketch, overall it is designed to pack a hard punch, using the theme of bullying and its long-term effects. Rob has no redeeming qualities; Simon, having seen the tragic consequences, is repentant.

Of the three roles, Rob and Simon need strong character performances. Apart from a few cries for help, Kenny is a non-speaking part, and he remains 'faceless', with his back to the audience.

If a school is doing any sort of push on a bullying policy, this will fit in perfectly.

YOU WILL NEED
- a chair
- a bottle filled with water
- a bag

SCRIPT: (KENNY *is sitting centre stage, back to audience.* ROB *and* SIMON *enter, they are unaware of* KENNY.)

ROB: Hold yer horses, Si. I don't understand what the point of this is. Why have you brought us here? Simon?

SIMON: Brings back memories, don't it?

ROB: Yeah, I suppose—now let's go.

SIMON: Nearly 20 years, but it still comes flooding back.

ROB: That's what memories tend to do—now come on.

SIMON: I had my first kiss over there.

ROB: Where?

SIMON: Behind the bike shed, believe it or not. Sounds like a cliché, but it's true. Amy Saunders.

ROB: You got a snog out of Amy Saunders!

SIMON: No, not a snog. We were only seven at the time. Just a little peck, but I tell you it felt good. I can remember it like it was yesterday. It all started when her best friend Claire Bridges uttered those immortal words . . .

ROB: (*Becomes Claire Bridges.*) 'Scuse me, but my mate fancies you.

SIMON: (*Becomes younger self.*) Eh?

ROB: My mate Amy Saunders fancies you.

SIMON: So what?

ROB: She wants to kiss you.

SIMON: UGGHH! She's a . . . girl!

ROB: 'Course she's a girl!

SIMON: Yuk! I don't wanna kiss a girl.

ROB: Why not?

SIMON: 'Cos . . . 'cos they all smell.

ROB: Ugh, that means you like kissing boys.

SIMON: No I don't!

ROB: Do.

SIMON: DON'T!

ROB: DO!

SIMON: DON'T!

ROB: Prove it then.

SIMON: How?

ROB: Kiss Amy Saunders . . .

(*Revert to original characters.*)

SIMON: So to prove my seven-year-old masculinity, I tasted Amy Saunders' ruby red lips under the watchful eye of Claire Bridges behind that very same bike shed, over 20 years ago.

ROB: And as future years proved, you were the first of many—very many! Are you ready to go now?

SIMON: That must have been about the same time we started our reign of terror.

ROB: Oh Simon, don't do this.

SIMON: Only in a small way to start with, maybe.

ROB: If it helps you, Si, give me the blame. I take full responsibility.

SIMON: NO! I could have stopped you but I didn't. I just stood by and watched . . . and then joined in. Well, why not? He was an easy target, wasn't he, Kenny Regis?

ROB: We were just kids, Si. Kids can be cruel, it's a sad fact of life. We were just kids . . .

(ROB *and* SIMON *become their seven-year-old selves.* KENNY *is now visible*.)

ROB: Stinky, smelly Kenny. Stinky, smelly Kenny! Everybody hates him 'cos he's a big fat benny.

SIMON: Yeah, you're a big fat benny, Kenny.

ROB: Your mum's a fat old bag and she smells too.

SIMON: Yeah, your whole family smells of poo.

ROB: And you wet your bed and the whole school hates you.

SIMON: You smell of wee and poo and everybody hates you!

ROB: Even the teachers hate you. Miss Wilton said, 'I hate that Kenny Regis 'cos he's a big smelly benny.' And she said you'll never have any friends, or ever get married or have children, and everyone will always hate you . . . (*Both slap and hit* KENNY.) Now give us your lunch money, Kenny. Smelly, benny Kenny . . .

KENNY: (*High-pitched squeal.*) Stop, stop, STOP!

(*Short pause, then* ROB *and* SIMON *revert to original characters.*)

ROB: We were just kids, Simon.

SIMON: Can't you admit you were wrong, Rob, even now?

ROB: What do you want me to say?

SIMON: Eight years it carried on. Were we still just kids at 15? Remember that school disco, the one where I reacquainted myself with Amy? The one where we finished Kenny off—I mean really finished him off . . .

(*Background 80s music plays.* SIMON *becomes his 15-year-old self*, ROB *is Amy Saunders. They are slow dancing.*)

ROB: 'Ere, watch your 'ands, mate—I ain't that easy!

SIMON: Oh come on, Ames, loosen up a bit. You know I love you.

ROB: Yeah right, Si. You know all about love at 15.

SIMON: But I'm well mature for my age. Everyone says so.

ROB: Whatever . . . Oh look over there. Kenny Regis sitting on his own in the corner. I feel a bit sorry for him. I don't think he's got any friends.

SIMON: That's 'cos he's a right saddo. You wait till I find Rob . . . ROB!

(ROB *becomes his 15-year-old self.*)

BOTH: KENNY NO MATES! KENNY NO MATES!

ROB: Ah, look who it is, Si. Our best mate Kenny. Ooh, I wonder if I can squeeze past all his hundreds of friends. Enjoy the party, did you, Kenny?

SIMON: Did you get a snog, Kenny?

ROB: Smelly Kenny.

SIMON: Smelly Kenny the benny! (*They are in hysterics.*)

ROB: Want some vodka—I mean cream soda? . . . Answer me then, you freak! (*Throws vodka in* KENNY's *face.*) You're pathetic!

SIMON: A waste of space.

ROB: I don't know how I put up with your miserable, ugly little face.

SIMON: Oh, I think he's wet himself, Rob.

ROB: Ugghh! It's disgusting. Maybe we should put him out of his misery. No friends, no birds, no life, no future. It would be kindest really.

(ROB *smacks* KENNY's *face;* SIMON *copies him. There follows a short, sharp, violent choreographed one-way fight, in which* ROB *and* SIMON *brutally pummel* KENNY. *After a series of blows* KENNY *falls to floor utterly defeated.* KENNY *should always have his back to the audience. There is a silent pause as* ROB *and* SIMON *look down at the sobbing* KENNY. ROB *and* SIMON *revert to adult characters.*)

ROB: We were just kids, Si.

SIMON: He never did have any real friends. Never had a girlfriend, never moved away from home. Bit of a loner.

ROB: Well some people are like that—it's life.

SIMON: But we made him like that, don't you see?

ROB: No, I don't. Now are you coming or not?

SIMON: Sorry.

ROB: What?

SIMON: Sorry. That's what his suicide note read. Just sorry.

ROB: What was that then? A message to his mum or a description of his life?

SIMON: You just don't care, do you?

ROB: No, I don't. I never did like him. Why should I pretend now?

SIMON: So why come to the funeral?

ROB: Seemed like the right thing to do. I thought we might have a bit of a laugh. Wish I hadn't bothered. Oh, I'll see you back in the pub. (ROB *exits*.)

SIMON: I don't know if you can hear me, Kenny.

(KENNY *retakes his opening position*.)

SIMON: I had the power to make things different, but I was a stupid little coward. I stood by and let it all happen. I joined in, I admit that. For what it's worth, I'm sorry. I'm really sorry . . .

(SIMON *exits*.)

TEACHING POINT: When you see someone suffering at the hands of another, don't turn your back. Step in and help them.

BIBLE REFERENCE: Proverbs 24:9.

APPLICATION: Moral teaching on bullying. God expects us to show compassion and love for others.

CHINESE MIMES

THEME: Communication.

INTRODUCTION: Using a slightly modern twist on the old parlour game, Chinese Whispers, this assembly should create some laughter and a good platform for the challenge.

   Anything goes in the mime section, so be prepared! The good news is that the more of a mess the mimes are, the funnier it is and better for the message.

   This idea would work best with smaller assemblies. Where it is impractical to send pupils out of the room, they could be stood behind a folding screen and the mime instructions written on large A1 card for all except the contestants to see.

OUTLINE: Select five volunteers and number them one to five. Send numbers two to five out of the room. Decide on a phrase to mime. To include the rest of the assembly, I suggest you think of three ideas, then have a vote to choose one. A couple of suggestions might be a ballet-dancing elephant or Elvis Presley eating a sandwich. Anything equally odd will serve the purpose.

Call in number two, and number one attempts to mime the phrase for 30 seconds. Regardless of how it's going they should mime for the complete time.

While number two quickly thinks what it could be (strictly no conferring), call in number three and so on until you reach number five. In effect, one mimes to two, two to three, and so on down the line. The mimes should cause much hilarity.

Next, go down the line and ask each volunteer what they honestly thought the mime was and how they communicated it to the next in line. This should show how easy it is for communication to break down.

Initiate some applause and award prizes.

Now link into how often in life communication breaks down. Someone tells another person to tell someone else, the message is misunderstood and things go pear-shaped! The way to avoid problems like this is to cut out the middleman where possible and find out things from the original source.

TEACHING POINT: Find out about God, direct from the Bible.

BIBLE REFERENCE: Psalm 119:19.

APPLICATION: Link this to the message that many people talk about God, Jesus and Christianity, but the best way to find out the truth is to go direct to the original source and read the Bible.

CABIN CREW

THEME: Arrogance.

INTRODUCTION: This one is for anyone who has ever had a bit of a giggle during the safety announcements on an aeroplane. It always amazes me how so many people totally ignore them, preferring to chat or read the in-flight magazine. I find the information incredibly entertaining, and let's be honest, it's pretty important too.

By turning a couple of assembly volunteers into the school's very own cabin crew, you'll raise a few laughs and introduce the theme of arrogance and its dangers.

YOU WILL NEED
- suitable airline props, such as life jacket
- prizes

OUTLINE: To begin, tell the assembly how much you love air travel. Get a show of hands as to who's been on an aeroplane, and share a personal anecdote about air travel. If you like, you can borrow one of mine! I was on a plane a few years back and the girl next to me grabbed me in a sudden wave of panic, announcing there was smoke billowing out from the engine. I immediately looked, totally calm of course, and was relieved to inform her that it wasn't smoke, but clouds!

Go on to say how you enjoy the cabin crew's safety announcements. Then instead of explaining them further, ask for the help of one boy and one girl.

Once on stage, tell them you want their help to re-enact the announcements on an aeroplane. (If you can, get hold of any props or costumes like life jacket, safety belt or hat, as this would be a bonus.)

Next put on an announcer's voice and read a safety message, prompting the volunteers to provide suitable actions. They'll probably need some jostling and encouragement. Create your own script based on directions to nearest exits, how to put on a life jacket and inflate it, the use of oxygen masks and, of course, the all-important lifesaving whistle!

Encourage applause for the brave volunteers and give them a prize as they return to their seats.

Go on to tell the assembly how amazed you are during air travel that no one takes any notice of the announcements. People are chatting, fiddling with their headphones, reading books and magazines, picking their noses or checking their sick bag is new! The arrogance! Imagine if there was an accident, there would be hysteria and no one would have a clue where to go. (Except the cabin crew, who would probably be thinking, 'Serves you all right!')

Link this to how we can so easily be arrogant, thinking we know it all and being unwilling to be told things that are for our own good.

TEACHING POINT: Wise people are informed people.

BIBLE REFERENCE: Proverbs 8:33.

APPLICATION: If desired, you can further link this to a more overt Christian message. God, through his Son Jesus, is in effect giving an important life-saving safety announcement. Jesus himself says, 'I am the way, the truth and the life.' Yet some turn from this, saying it's not important or not for them. For such a major decision in your life, are you sure you are fully informed?

BABBLE

THEMES: Prayer, communication, listening.

INTRODUCTION: Volumes of books have been written about prayer and communicating with God, so even trying to touch on this subject in a short assembly is pretty hard. However, we can deal with single aspects of the larger picture.

Most teenagers love to talk, and that can often be a pain, but for this assembly you need to find a pair who could talk for England! After giving them a speaking challenge that is much harder than it first seems, you can look at the topic of what communicating with God really is (and isn't!).

YOU WILL NEED
- two chairs
- a stopwatch
- prizes

OUTLINE: Introduce the assembly by reminding people of that famous old cliché that we have two ears and one mouth, so we should listen twice as much as we speak. Explain that when you were younger you hated this advice and much preferred talking. Get a show of hands to see who prefers, on the whole, talking to listening.

Now say that you need to find the two champion talkers in the assembly—the boy and the girl with the biggest mouth. This should cause some fun and much finger-pointing. Select your two volunteers, perhaps taking advice from the teachers, and get them on stage.

Depending on time this game can have one or two rounds as follows. In the first round, each talker in turn is given a topic to speak on for as long as they can without pausing. They are shown the topic, given five seconds' thinking space, then timed for as long as they manage to speak. Make the topics very general: film, music, sport, holidays, school. The winner is obviously the one who lasts longest.

An optional second round is for them to have a head-to-head challenge. They are both given the same topic and, with seats facing, they talk on that subject over the top of each other. The winner is the one who lasts longest.

It is essential to have a few spare subjects, as with nerves and laughter it can take a couple of attempts before they get going.

Initiate applause and award prizes as necessary.

Now explain that the game, so excellently played by your volunteers, was all about talking, or one-way communication. Real communication, however, is two-way, listening and speaking, yet in reality we often prefer to do just the talking.

TEACHING POINT: Prayer is two-way communication.

BIBLE REFERENCE: Psalm 66:16–20.

APPLICATION: For a Christian, prayer is communicating with God. It's not just about spinning off a list of requests: 'Please, God, give me this, that and the other; make so and so well; help such and such a team win the football; make so and so fancy me!' It is about asking for things and giving thanks for things, but it's also about listening to what God might be trying to tell us. If appropriate, close in prayer, thanking God, praising God and asking him to speak into our hearts and situations.

LEARNING FROM MISTAKES

THEME: Mistakes.

INTRODUCTION: It's not easy having to admit you're wrong, that you've made a mistake or that you lost, but at the end of the day it's part of life and we can't be totally protected from it.

My nephew recently took part in a school sports day, but there were no races or competitive events. It was deemed that the taking part was of sole importance. Worthy as that thinking is, I think it's taking things a bit too far. Surely there's an important lesson in not simply winning or losing, but how we deal with the inevitability of sometimes not coming out on top.

By running a very basic competition, in this assembly you can provoke some thoughts on our attitudes to winning and losing.

YOU WILL NEED
- a jar of coins (or your preferred substitute prop)
- prizes

OUTLINE: Tell the assembly you wish to think about winners and losers and aim to run a simple competition, for which you need some volunteers. Depending on the competition you use, select your volunteers, probably around four.

Display a jar full of coins and ask everyone to predict how much they think is in the jar. After a short pause ask each of your volunteers one at a time what their prediction is.

Next ask the whole assembly what they think, saying that on the count of three you want them to shout out their predictions! After the cacophony of noise has died down, thank the assembly, saying that you just about managed to take all that information in!

Announce the actual amount, and award a prize to whoever was nearest from your chosen volunteers. You can also ask the assembly if anyone was spot on—it makes no odds either way, but it's quite amusing, as some bright spark is bound to chirp up.

Now go on to explain how it's frustrating in life when we get things wrong, maybe in a test, in a relationship or in a choice we make. Give some examples of people who have been wrong:

- When J. K. Rowling wrote the first Harry Potter book, several publishers turned it down.
- Albert Einstein was asked to leave school because his teachers thought he would never amount to anything.
- Perhaps use a personal story of a time when you got something disastrously wrong.

The important thing to remember is that we are human, and at one time or another we all make mistakes. If we set ourselves the unattainable target of always being right, we are eventually going to be very disappointed. It is key to make sure we learn from the mistakes we make to avoid the same thing happening again; and in the times we are right or win, we should do so in a gracious manner.

TEACHING POINT: How to cope with winning and losing.

BIBLE REFERENCE: 2 Corinthians 13:5–7.

APPLICATION: If you wish, develop the Christian message by talking about how God can forgive us and turn our mistakes around.

KICK THE HABIT

THEMES: Habits, Holy Spirit.

INTRODUCTION: The idea of this assembly is to introduce the theme of the power habits can have over us, and how they easily become part and parcel of who we are. It has been said of the church, which is steeped in ritual, that you only need to do something once and it automatically becomes tradition!

The slight twist to this illustration is that instead of focusing on bad habits, as would be expected in an assembly, we also communicate that good habits can be hard to break too. So our behaviour patterns can have positive results.

Note: It would be wise to seek the school's advice on who to choose as a volunteer for this assembly.

YOU WILL NEED
- a thin sheet of paper
- a length of balsa wood
- a metal bar (or something unbreakable)

OUTLINE: Open by telling the assembly what a fan you are of martial arts films or anything with kick boxing in it. Ask if there are any kick boxers in the assembly. If there are, ask if they would be a willing volunteer, or if not ask for a volunteer who is willing to have a go. Initiate some applause for the brave volunteer.

Once you have your volunteer tell them you're going to start easy and work your way up! Their first test is a piece of thin paper. With the help of a second person, hold out a long strip of paper and challenge the volunteer to kick through it in as impressive a way as possible. Of course they will succeed.

The second challenge is the same but with a length of balsa wood. To ensure they succeed you can score down the middle for a most impressive effect! It doesn't matter if it takes a couple of goes. In fact, it makes your point better. Encourage some enthusiastic support for the volunteer.

For the third challenge get out a metal bar, or anything that is unbreakable. Let the volunteer have a couple of tries, as long as they are wearing reasonable footwear, but make sure they don't go too mad and injure themselves! They will fail this time, but give them a prize and prompt some encouragement as they take their seat.

Now ask everyone to think of a habit they have that seems very hard to break. At first they could take it or leave it; it could be broken as easily as kicking through paper. Then it got a bit more routine, although they probably could have broken it with a bit more effort, like kicking through the wood. Eventually, though, the habit became an addiction, and now, even if they wanted to, it has become virtually impossible to break, like trying to work your way through the metal.

Whether our habit is a health risk like smoking, or a social risk like spending hours on computer games, the more we allow it to become routine, the harder it will be to break its cycle of control.

Go on to say that when most people think of habits, they think of bad things. But habits can also be good. As bad as it can be to allow negative behaviour to get a hold on us, it can be positive to allow good and kind things to become a habit. So what are your habits, good or bad, and are you in control of them?

TEACHING POINT: Are you in control of your habits, or are they in control of you?

BIBLE REFERENCE: Romans 7:5–16.

APPLICATION: Through our conscience, God lets us know what we need to do and what we should avoid. He gives us the strength and ability to break the power that habits have over us.

IT'S NO SACRIFICE

THEMES: Sacrifice, relationships, materialism.

INTRODUCTION: It is highly unlikely that many teenagers will have had experience of making any great sacrifices. It is true, though, that we will all need to make certain sacrifices at one time or another, some big and some small.

Using volunteers to stage an illustration and a popular Bible story, we can raise some thought-provoking pointers to what kinds of sacrifice we think we would or would not be prepared to make.

YOU WILL NEED
- sacrifice cards (as explained in Outline section below)

OUTLINE: Open the assembly by asking people to think of a time in their lives when they have had to make a sacrifice of some kind. Maybe someone had to move because of a parent's job and leave close friends behind. Maybe someone had to forego a holiday, as the dates clashed with an important event at home. Maybe people can't really think of anything that has so far caused them to make any kind of sacrifice, but whether it's something they've experienced or not, at certain times as life goes by we are all called to make certain sacrifices.

Give an example of a sacrifice you have made. For me, I left a pretty well-paid and secure job to move into a line of work I was passionate about but which paid less. Alternatively, you could make the same point by recalling a time you were challenged to make a sacrifice but for whatever reason refused. For instance, ending a relationship because of the geographical move that would be necessary to continue. As another alternative, you could use a current media story with a theme of sacrifice.

Now choose two volunteers, one male and one female, to illustrate a point. Explain to your volunteers that they are deeply in love with one another. (You can milk this a bit as it's bound to get some reaction.) Bearing that in mind, what would they be willing to sacrifice if asked to by the other?

Display six sacrifice cards, which the volunteers take turns in randomly selecting. Here are some ideas you could use:

- Fashion sense.
- A job that is too time-consuming.
- The desire to have children.
- Need to move geographical location.
- 'Unhelpful' friends.
- Your life!

In turn ask the volunteers, remembering they are pretending to be totally in love, which of their selections they would be prepared to sacrifice and why. The results will be interesting and often amusing.

Link this to a brief retelling of the story of the Rich Young Man found in Matthew 19:16–30. Highlight the biblical message that Jesus asked the man to sacrifice the one thing he held dear, which of course is the central point of making a sacrifice. (It's not much of a sacrifice to give up doing the washing-up!)

Conclude by challenging the assembly as to what they would be willing to sacrifice and for whom.

TEACHING POINT: The meaning of sacrifice.

BIBLE REFERENCE: Matthew 19:16–30.

APPLICATION: For teaching on the gospel message, you can link this to the Christian belief that Christ made the ultimate sacrifice when he died on the cross. Compared to this, any sacrifice we make pales into insignificance.

TO VOTE OR NOT TO VOTE

THEMES: Voting, governments, democracy.

INTRODUCTION: This assembly will work particularly well at election time, but it can be used effectively at any time. In society at present there is a high degree of apathy when it comes to elections, politics and politicians. This is especially true of our young people. So if we live in a time of mass disillusion over whether politics can ever serve our greater need, is it worth protecting the hard-fought-for democracy we live in?

YOU WILL NEED
- acetates of pictures of the current main party leaders
- acetates of popular excuses for not voting

OUTLINE: Open by asking the assembly for their initial thoughts when you mention the word 'politics'. Get some responses from the floor (they are likely to be on the negative side).

Now challenge them on how much they know about politics, starting with a very easy picture quiz. Show pictures of the main party leaders and possibly some extra cabinet ministers: the chancellor, education secretary, etc . . .

Explain that we live in a democratic country, which means everybody from the age of 18 has the right to register and vote. This gives us the right to elect our leaders: we can have our say, unlike many other countries. Brilliant! What an amazing privilege . . . or maybe not.

Incredibly, it is true that in the UK only a small minority of the population elects many of today's governments, because for one reason or another people choose not to vote.

Now run a mock election. Explain to the assembly that they have to decide how and if they would vote given the chance this morning. They will be asked to stand to one of the following choices: Labour, Conservative, Lib. Dem., other or wouldn't vote. You can expand on each of the choices, obviously being careful not to reveal your own personal choice.

Draw a conclusion from the result. If most voted for the 'wouldn't vote' choice, explain that they mirror the average election. If they did vote, congratulate them on the effort made.

Now say how it seems surprising that people choose not to use their democratic right to vote and you are going to look at some of the common reasons for this. Put these up on the screen. They can include:

- Foregone conclusion.
- Haven't got the time.
- Doesn't make any difference who wins as they're all the same.
- All politicians are corrupt.
- One vote won't make any difference.

Add a bit of flesh to these opinions, explaining how such attitudes would amaze people who live in countries where they have no such rights, or if they do will walk and queue for hours to cast their vote.

Conclude by saying what a great privilege we have to be free to vote for whoever we want, and for that we should be grateful. If we don't bother to vote it seems a bit ridiculous to then complain about the government that is put in place. Democracy only really works properly if everyone plays his or her part.

TEACHING POINT: The importance of protecting our democracy.

BIBLE REFERENCE: Proverbs 8:15.

APPLICATION: Christians believe in a God of justice and freedom, who gives help to the oppressed.

A MORAL CONUNDRUM

KS2 KS3 KS4

THEMES: Moral judgements, appearances, prejudice.

INTRODUCTION: A key directive of the Department for Education and Skills is to provide opportunity for a child's moral development. In this assembly we attempt to do just that, testing individuals in a non-threatening way as to how they make moral judgements.

What is most important in a person? Is it how they look, what they do or who they are?

YOU WILL NEED
• acetates with pictures of various people

OUTLINE: Open by saying that you're sure everyone has heard the saying 'Never judge a book by its cover'. It's a bit of a cliché, and we may find it rather annoying, but all the same it is true.

Go on to say how it's never more true than when referring to how we make snap judgements about other people, often simply based on their outward appearance.

Now show a series of acetates depicting famous and not so famous people, asking the assembly to think about what their first impression would be. These can be of anyone, but include faces from a variety of social strata.

For the main illustration, say you are going to test everyone on how they come to make moral judgements. Imagine a hypothetical scenario, where there has been a nuclear or chemical war and you are in a shelter with three other people. Supplies are low and it has been decided that only two people can realistically survive. Who of the following three would you elect to keep?

Choose three to use from the following list, or make up your own, but at this point only give the briefest description: supermodel, politician, footballer, vicar, blind man, seven-year-old child, upper-class lady.

Give the assembly a few moments to decide who they would keep and why. Gather a few opinions from some chosen volunteers.

For the twist, add a second round by fleshing out the original descriptions to see if that changes anyone's perceptions. For instance, the supermodel is male! (This usually flummoxes most of the lads.) The upper-class lady has a cure for nuclear- or chemical-related diseases. The blind man was a dealer in nuclear arms.

Again, give a few moments for people to appraise the new information, then check the volunteers' opinions to see if there are any changes.

Close by saying how important it is that we don't 'judge a book by its cover', but that we are prepared to find out more about people before we make any snap judgements.

TEACHING POINT: Don't be influenced by appearances.

BIBLE REFERENCE: 1 Samuel 16:7.

APPLICATION: People judge on appearances but God looks at the heart.

A BUNCH OF PHOBIAS

THEMES: Fear, empathy.

INTRODUCTION: When compiling this book I thought it would be good to include a piece on overcoming fear and having empathy with others in the areas where they struggle. In my search I turned to the trusty Internet, and was amazed at what I found!

Looking at a myriad of phobias ranging from the sublime to the totally ridiculous, this assembly should cause the students to put their fears into perspective and to help them to understand those of others. You can also link into the Christian message about the strength to face fear that God gives.

YOU WILL NEED
• pre-prepared acetates with different fears listed

OUTLINE: Begin the assembly by stating how complex humans are, and that everyone in the world is different. To prove the point, quickly throw out some random questions to the assembly, choosing various people to answer. The answers should all be different, but if not just make light of it. Questions can include: 'What's your favourite television programme; music; band; film star?' Alternatively, you can be a bit more personal and ask, 'What makes you happy; sad; angry?' Finish with the question, 'What makes you frightened?'

Now comment on how it's odd that one person can be absolutely petrified of something, whereas another person will remain totally unaffected. I recently saw the film *Eight-Legged Freaks*! Because I'm so totally unbothered by spiders it had no effect on me whatsoever. Many around me in the cinema, however, were squealing and writhing in their seats.

Add to this the thought that it is totally inappropriate to say to others how silly their fear is, because they can't help it. Now show a list of well-known fears and phobias to see if the students can guess what they are. To make it more interesting, show them an acetate with some kind of pictorial visual to illustrate the fear.

Common fears
• Arachnophobia—spiders.
• Necrophobia—death or dead things.
• Astraphobia—thunder and lightning.
• Claustrophobia—confined spaces.
• Agoraphobia—open spaces.
• Sociophobia—people.

Unusual fears
• Ablutophobia—washing or bathing.
• Cacophobia—ugliness.
• Didaskaleinophobia—going to school.
• Ecclesiophobia—church.
• Ephebiophobia—teenagers.
• Gamophobia—marriage.
• Peladophobia—bald people.

Wacky fears!
- Arachibutyophobia—peanut butter sticking to the top of your mouth!
- Hippopotomonstroseguppedaliophobia—long words!

(Honest! It was all on the Internet, so it must be true!)

Now say that although some of these seem daft, different people have different fears. In the same way that we want people to respect and support our often irrational fears, we must try to understand and empathise with others too. Ultimately we defeat our fears when we feel secure, but this is hard. Someone who is afraid of snakes will still be scared even if the snake is behind three feet of bullet-proof glass!

TEACHING POINT: It is important to overcome our fears by facing up to them.

BIBLE REFERENCE: Psalm 56:3.

APPLICATION: Further link this to the Christian belief that God helps us to overcome our fears. They don't simply go away as if by magic, but the more we entrust our fears to God, he helps us through.

PART TWO

CULTURAL DEVELOPMENT

VINCE THE LAD

THEMES: Poverty, Third World need.

INTRODUCTION: I originally wrote this monologue to perform at a presentation highlighting issues surrounding Third World need. Vince is a typical 19-year-old lad: into football, women and booze. As such he may seem a strange choice of character to highlight poverty, but it is because he is so unlikely that he challenges us all. Although we care about poverty, do we care enough to do anything about it?

With a strong caricature performance, this works well in assemblies, introducing the theme of our response and responsibility to the Third World.

YOU WILL NEED
- a suitable costume (Ben Sherman shirt, baggy jeans, Doc Marten boots . . .)

(*The sketch opens with loud music blasting.* VINCE *stands centre stage, frozen. When the music stops, he begins.*)

SANDRA! Stone the crows, woman, get a shift on . . . Sandra!

(*To audience.*) I dunno about all this political correctness lark that's going round at the moment, but I tell ya—there's nothing I like more than standing at the top of my ladder, giving my windows a good chamois, looking down at all them lovely ladies and calling out in my best Queen's English, 'OI OI OI, HOWZABOUT IT THEN, DARLIN'?, Eh eh eh!' Don't get me wrong. I don't think them right-wing feminists are a big fan, but most of the girls who walk down the Islington High Street absolutely love it!

For instance, take Sandra, my new bird. Fell prey to my charms a few months back. Now boys, listen and learn. I chatted her up one lunchtime when I was doing the windows of the building society she works at, right? That same evening I treated her out to an à la carte doner kebab, invited her back to my gaff, stuck me greatest hits of Madness CD on and knocked her sideways, no problem. I dunno how I manage it. I must be a natural or summink!

Anyway, my boys I hang out with—the Highbury Mafia they call us—a right bunch of desperadoes or what! They couldn't pull a bird if she had one arm and a winch! 'Vince,' they say. 'Vince, how do you do it with all the birds, mate?' 'I dunno,' I say. 'I think it's all got to do with animal magnetism!' The only reason why such a suave and sophisticated guy as me hangs out with that bunch of yobbish losers is for our Saturday afternoon soirées at Highbury Stadium. We all pile in the north stand, sink a few pints, have a bit of a laugh, kick a few away supporters' heads in. Can't be bad. I tell ya, there's nothing like the ringing sound of your Doc Marten boot connecting with the head of a Man United supporter—lovely! You might think it all sounds a bit violent, but it's only a bit of a laugh, innit! Blimey, where's it got to? (*Shouts up the stairs.*) SANDRA!

She's up there at the mo, tarting herself up with her best mate Vicky. Vicky, who wears skirts the width of a bit of dental floss, applies her make-up with a trowel and just about managed to scrape one GCSE in needlework. Still, I can't complain about my Sandra. She's a good girl—brought me a lovely present this afternoon. A new Ben Sherman shirt and a bottle of the old Paco Rabanne. Once I've got that lot on I'll be sorted. She said to me the other day (*impersonates Sandra*), 'Ooh Vince, do you know why I love you so much?' Well I would have answered, but it could have been one of a thousand things, so I let it go on. (*Continues impression.*) 'I love you 'cos you're such a sensitive man!'

Now I wouldn't of thought of that, but give it a bit of credit, she's quite right, 'cos I am in touch with my more caring and feminine side. Example, last Friday I treated her to a slap-up fish 'n' chip supper. Now I only got about halfway through mine 'cos me guts were giving me a bit of gyp (my own fault—I'd had six pints and a dodgy curry the night before). Anyway, Miss Sarky Moo says, 'Ooh, what a waste! There's millions starving in Africa who'd give their right arm for that.' So without thinking, and in hindsight rather stupidly, I chucked it at her and said, 'Well send it to 'em then!'

Now as soon as I said it I realised how daft it sounded, 'cos it's not really practical to shove a half-eaten tray of haddock, chips and mushy peas into a jiffy bag and send it to Africa. For a start, who would you send it to? Genghis Khan? Muppetma Gandhi? Winston Mandela? No, so as a compromise I took it home, bunged it in the blender and served it up as a treat for my cute pit bull called Sultan. He loved it.

But back to my caring and feminine side. You see, the whole thing's been playing on my mind ever since. I mean, think about it: all the spare food that's kicking around that nobody wants or needs—why can't they be sent it? Not in dribs and drabs in Jiffy bags, but you know, as a big job lot like. I suppose it's all got to do with political sanitations, butter mountains and the export price of bananas. Not that a starving family would give two hoots about all that. Still, what can you do about it? Well, there's nothing you *can* do, is there? . . . SANDRA!

TEACHING POINT: Our response and responsibility to the Third World.

BIBLE REFERENCE: Proverbs 22:9.

APPLICATION: The importance of helping others in need, and Christian teaching on giving aid.

FEEDING THE FIVE MILLION

THEMES: Poverty, Third World need.

INTRODUCTION: This short sketch works well and can lead thought in two directions. As well as easily giving the opportunity to link into the cultural issues of Third World need and famine, it also gives a springboard into the age-old question of why God is apparently willing to watch millions starve without intervening.

Drawing on the miracle of the feeding of the five thousand, this sketch shifts the onus onto us to make a difference in the world.

YOU WILL NEED
- a chocolate bar

SCRIPT: (ONE *is moody and cynical;* TWO *is much more laid back. As they enter,* ONE *is stuffing a chocolate bar in their mouth.*)

ONE: What a complete load of tripe.

TWO: What's up with you?

ONE: He must think we're all completely doolally!

TWO: Who? What are you talking about?

ONE: That vicar. Drivelling on about Jesus feeding 5,000 people.

TWO: Well, what's wrong with that?

ONE: Come on—didn't you hear him? (*Adopting stereotypical vicar voice.*) So Jesus did taketh the little boyeth's five loaveths and two fisheths, and verily he did waveth his magic wandeth, and lo and behold there was enough for five thousand greedy piggeths to stuffeth their faces fulleth . . . (*Reverting to own voice.*) What a complete pile of poopeth! I mean, call me foolish, but under ordinary circumstances it just doesn't happen, does it? (*Takes a bite from his chocolate bar.*)

TWO: Well no, I'll give you that. Under ordinary circumstances it doesn't. But this was a miracle of course, and a miracle by its very nature has to be extraordinary. If the story was about Jesus sharing a 17-pound turkey between a dozen people, it wouldn't exactly be a miracle, would it?

ONE: I suppose I see what you mean . . .

TWO: So what's the problem then?

ONE: Well, I'll tell you what the crux of the problem is. It's all very well hearing stories 2,000 years old about Jesus feeding 5,000 people just 'cos they couldn't be bothered to go home for their tea, but here we are, a supposedly advanced society, and half the world's dying of starvation. If Jesus is so loving and wonderful, why can't he feed them?

TWO: Fair point. World starvation is a major problem. But if you think back to the story, Jesus didn't magically make the food appear from nowhere, did he? No, he used what the boy offered.

ONE: What! A piffling little bit of bread and fish?

TWO: It wasn't piffling at all. That boy gave Jesus all he had. You imagine if the world adopted the same attitude today. God has provided enough food on this earth to feed us all until we're completely stuffed, with loads to spare. The problem isn't that God doesn't care or provide, it's that we're too greedy to share.

ONE: (*Guiltily puts his chocolate away.*) Well, I s'pose so.

TWO: Just imagine the impact if individuals, governments and nations captured the real message of this simple story. It would be more than a few thousand that would be fed; it would be countless millions. Do you think that would be an ordinary circumstance?

ONE: No mate, it would be a flippin' miracle!

TEACHING POINT: When we make sacrifices, we will see miracles.

BIBLE REFERENCE: John 6:1–15.

APPLICATION: Can be used to make both spiritual and cultural points.

A BIG CHUNK OF CHOCOLATE

  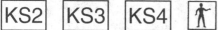

KS2 KS3 KS4

THEMES: Poverty, Third World, wealth, aid.

INTRODUCTION: Having spent a few years working for a Third World missionary aid organisation, I unsurprisingly have an interest in the enormous gap between the wealth of the richest and poorest countries. The vast majority of our population would consider themselves to be concerned for the plight of other countries, but how much do we really care if it means any kind of change in our living conditions?

In this assembly we attempt to raise awareness of the great gulf in wealth, and what our response should be. This idea could be simplified and used effectively with KS1.

YOU WILL NEED
• a large bar of chocolate

OUTLINE: Introduce the assembly by showing either a video clip or some still images of current Third World plight. Explain that these images are common around the world, and pose the question, 'Do we really care?'

Expand on this point by giving the difference between passive and active caring. Most humans don't enjoy watching such misery and, in the comfort of their own homes, are saddened by such images. This is passive caring. Active caring is where the sadness caused by obvious injustice stirs us into some kind of action.

Now give these interesting facts from the United Nations human development report:

- 250 years ago, the richest countries in the world were at most five times richer than the poorest.
- In 1976 Switzerland was 52 times richer than Mozambique. In 1997 that had increased to 508 times richer! The gap is widening and fast.

Now ask for six volunteers to perform this illustration:

- Two represent a rich First World country, e.g. USA or Switzerland.
- Two represent a Second World country, e.g. an Eastern European country like Romania or Ukraine.
- Two represent a Third World country in Africa, maybe Mozambique or any other currently in the news.

You can use this illustration in different ways, having more than three countries or the five continents, but for the practicalities of a large assembly it's best to keep it limited.

Take the bar of chocolate and announce that you're going to share it among the three teams. Now give the vast majority of the bar to the rich country, a few chunks to the Second World country and one chunk to the Third World country.

Explain that unfair as this seems, and there may well be some grumbling, this represents the disparity between the nations. But is this reasonable? This chocolate is to be shared among all their people, so what do they think should happen?

Give each team a minute or so to discuss their response to the situation. Will they ask for help? Will they offer help? Everyone else in the assembly should also discuss with their neighbours what they would do in this position.

After a minute ask for a few ideas from the general assembly, quizzing them on why they would do whatever they suggest. Be prepared for a wide range of responses.

Next ask the volunteers to explain what they would do, and see if any are prepared to share the chocolate. Again, of course, responses will vary, but on the whole the richer nations will usually be willing to share to a certain degree. Round up the illustration with a final thought, then thank the volunteers. Of course they get to keep the chocolate.

Close the assembly by saying that the United Nations recommends countries give a proportion of their wealth to poverty-stricken countries, but due to pressing home concerns few actually live up to this recommendation. Basically, people do care, but often not enough!

Note: This assembly will also work well as a lesson by dividing the class into the five continents and spending longer discussing the various implications in groups.

TEACHING POINT: Do you really care about Third World poverty?

BIBLE REFERENCE: Galatians 2:10.

APPLICATION: Discuss the importance of compassion and the fact that greed is wrong.

THIRD WORLD QUIZ

THEMES: Third World, poverty, aid.

INTRODUCTION: Here is another assembly attempting to raise awareness and provoke thought on issues related to Third World poverty, this time using an old favourite: the quiz. Have as much fun as you can with the quiz element, but ensure you allow some of the incredible facts 'air to breathe' and have a strong conclusion to tie things up at the end.

YOU WILL NEED
- questions on an acetate (optional)
- inflatable globe or beach ball
- chocolate bar prizes

OUTLINE: Open the assembly by saying that we think we know all about Third World plight—we see images on the television and read things in the paper—but in actual fact there is much we don't know; often things that are hidden on purpose.

Explain that you are going to have a multiple choice quiz and for each question the inflatable globe will be thrown or kicked into the assembly. Whoever catches it wins the right to answer and a correct answer wins a chocolate bar! (Encourage some enthusiastic whoops!)

I sourced my questions from the United Nations website, in particular the human development report, but you may have come upon some other staggering statistics and facts that you could use instead. Asterisks below denote correct answers.

1. It is estimated that how many people live in poverty?
    (a)   100 million
    (b)   1,000 million*
    (c)   10,000 million

2. What percentage of people in the majority world lack basic sanitation?
    (a)   10%
    (b)   30%
    (c)   60%*

3. What percentage of people in the majority world have no access to clean water?
    (a)   10%
    (b)   30%*
    (c)   40%

4. The 225 wealthiest people in the world have a combined wealth of how much?
    (a)   A thousand million dollars
    (b)   A million million dollars*
    (c)   Ten million million dollars

5. In Third World countries, which is the biggest killer among children?
    (a)   AIDS

(b)   Cancer

(c)   Diarrhoea*

6. The 20% of people living in the world's highest income countries consume approximately what percentage of the world's resources?

(a)   76%

(b)   86%*

(c)   96%

7. The United Nations recommends its member countries give 0.7% of their Gross National Product (GNP) to aid the poor. Only two countries currently manage this. Which ones are they?

(a)   USA and Canada

(b)   England and France

(c)   Netherlands and Sweden*

8. The USA spends approximately $2,765 per capita on private and public health. Second is Switzerland with $2,520 and third is Sweden with $2,343. How much is it in Mozambique?

(a) $5*

(b) $55

(c) $105

Close the quiz and express the desire that some of the answers have made people think about issues in the wider world. Finish the assembly by announcing the startling fact that if the 225 individuals mentioned in question 4, who have a combined wealth of a million million dollars, gave just 4% of their wealth (some $40 billion) it would be enough to provide basic education, healthcare, adequate food, safe water and sanitation for all the people of the world!

TEACHING POINT: Are the rich getting richer, while the poor get poorer?

BIBLE REFERENCE: Proverbs 3:9.

APPLICATION: Discuss the importance of compassion and the fact that greed is wrong.

ANNOYING TRUTHS

THEMES: Third World, poverty, social action.

INTRODUCTION: Continuing with our theme of Third World poverty, in this assembly we want to provoke a feeling of frustration or annoyance. The world doesn't always play with a fair deck and often the wool can be pulled over our eyes, with unfair practices being dressed up as great generosity.

Using a variety of facts and a participatory round of true and false, the message should be clear, and individual responses challenged.

YOU WILL NEED
• visuals/acetates for facts and questions

OUTLINE: Provoke the assembly at the beginning by saying that your aim this morning is to really frustrate and annoy all present. (If they know you, they may expect this anyway!)

Go on to say that the majority of humans have a sense of justice and fair play, and often things happen that we don't know about. Media coverage will often only show us one side of a story. Big corporations are often reluctant to advertise some of their market strategies and use of Third World labour/sweatshops. Politicians tend to let us know things only on a 'need to know' basis.

Produce this list of facts on Third World issues that although not hidden are also not advertised, saying that you hope they will annoy people. Communicate the following facts with a passion that betrays the sense of frustration you are seeking to foster.

- The world's production of grain alone could provide everyone in the world with the recommended 3,600 calories a day, yet people are still starving.
- Each year over 5 million people die from illnesses solely related to unclean water.
- What poor countries in Africa spend each year on debt repayment could save the lives of 3 million children and prevent a further million cases of malnutrition.

You could briefly expand on these or other similar statistics you come across. Next ask how these facts make people feel. Do they really care? Are they a bit sad, frustrated, annoyed, determined to cause a change?

Next tell the assembly that it's time for them to join in. Run a short true or false quiz, asking them to stand to vote for their answer.

- The average person in the UK consumes ten times more than a person in the Third World. (FALSE: it's 35 times more.)
- The British spend £1 billion per month on clothes. (FALSE, it's £2.5 billion.)
- 25% of food bought in Great Britain is thrown away. (TRUE.)
- One worker in a Third World country receives £1 for helping to make a pair of trainers costing £50. (FALSE: £1.19 is shared between 45 people.)
- One-fifth of the world's population receives 94% of the world's health services. (TRUE.)

Close by saying that abject poverty and starvation aren't only happening when we see them on our television screens; they are an ongoing problem. Are we prepared to make any sacrifices? Are we prepared in any way to get involved and try to make a change? Or are we happy to switch off the images and simply forget about them?

TEACHING POINT: What are we prepared to sacrifice to influence change?

BIBLE REFERENCE: Proverbs 14:21.

APPLICATION: God wants us to have compassion on those less fortunate.

PART THREE

SPIRITUAL DEVELOPMENT

ANARCHIC NOUGHTS AND CROSSES

THEME: Rules.

INTRODUCTION: This is a simple and highly visual illustration that makes a very clear point. You can use it in one of two ways, depending on the nature of your setting, the size of the hall, the number of people and preparation time available. Either draw large noughts and crosses grids on a wiper board or flip chart, choosing one boy and one girl for the challenge, or lay out nine chairs for the grid, and choose five boys and five girls for a physical version of the game. (This will obviously require more space and time to set up.)

YOU WILL NEED
- a large board with suitable writing implements

OR
- nine chairs set out in three rows of three

OUTLINE: As an introduction, explain that you weren't sure what to do to keep the assembly awake this morning, so for a bit of fun you decided to play a game, with the boys against the girls.

Next choose your volunteers, encouraging all the boys to cheer for the boys and the girls for the girls. (In a single sex school, simply split the hall down the middle.) Have a brief session of practising cheers and applause to liven things up.

Depending on time, play two or three games (they usually end in a draw, unless someone makes a really stupid mistake). Then call a halt, stating that it's all a bit boring and you suggest trying it a different way. From now on it's 'no rules' noughts and crosses! All the established and accepted rules, like taking it in turns, one symbol at a time, are out of the window and anarchy rules!

Let this sink in for a few seconds, then lead a backwards countdown to set anarchic noughts and crosses into action. The result should be an absolute mess. If written, the board will be one great scrawl; if physical, the chairs will be all over the place, bodies scattered! (Obviously you need to avoid World War 3, but allow a little pushing and shoving!) Ask the volunteers to sit back down and initiate some applause.

Link into a short talk, focusing the attention on what a mess resulted in there being no rules. Explain a scenario such as a football match with no rules or referee. The ball would constantly drift out of play, players would wander offside, and a big 22-man brawl would begin within five minutes! It all sounds funny, but in reality it would totally spoil the spirit of the match and make it worthless.

At this point, link to the importance of rules in society. Laws are put in place not just to restrict, but to protect. You can then develop this into a talk on school rules, society rules or biblical rules.

TEACHING POINT: Rules are put in place to protect, not restrict.

BIBLE REFERENCE: Exodus 20:1–21.

APPLICATION: Can be used as a general illustration on the importance of rules, or developed into teaching on the freedom given by God's rules. Explain how God's rules are for our protection. You can view the Ten Commandments as God waving his finger at us or loving us so much that he wants to protect us. Also explain that much is said about rules and what we can't do, but little is said about the huge freedom we have, with opportunities to do so much.

HAND IN GLOVE

THEMES: Purpose, creation.

INTRODUCTION: In all honesty this illustration is a bit of a silly one, but it does get a good laugh and you can make a good point about the purpose of human existence. It works best with younger age groups, but if you approach it enthusiastically it can be used with teenagers and even adults.

If possible use a few simple and creative props (costume, table with cloth, wand, etc.) to give the appearance that you are a talented magician. You will be pleased to know that you need absolutely no magic skills whatsoever!

YOU WILL NEED
- basic magician props (a table is the essential bare minimum)
- one glove (preferably a washing-up glove as for some reason Marigolds are very funny)

OUTLINE: To introduce this talk, explain to the assembly that you are a noted professional magician and you have a very special trick to show them! Now explain that with their help you will amaze them all by making a glove float in the air. At this point produce your glove and encourage some suitably astonished gasps.

Place the glove on the table and explain that you must all count to three, then hold out hands and together say 'Rise'. Give it a go.

The first effort will probably be pretty half-hearted and won't work. Jokingly complain that the trick needs everybody to be involved to make it succeed. Try again.

Surprise, surprise, it still didn't work! This time, pick on a couple of people who failed to join in, blaming them for the trick's failure.

On the third unsuccessful attempt, try to persuade some of the assembly that the little finger moved slightly. Of course it didn't and they will likely tell you this in no uncertain terms.

Before the final attempt, ask everyone to close their eyes. Be strict about this, picking on a few peekers, telling them not to open their eyes until you say. While their eyes are closed, put your hand in the glove, standing to the side to pretend you are not cheating. Invite the assembly to open their eyes and do the trick again, and this time bring your hand up to make the glove finally float!

At this point take a bow, seemingly impressed with your own brilliance. Expect some boos and calls of being a cheat. Invite a couple of people to tell you what they thought of the 'trick' and finally admit defeat.

To link to the message, explain that the reason you put your hand in the glove is because that is what gloves are for. A glove without a hand is totally pointless, useful for absolutely nothing. (As an alternative you can replace the glove with a shoe or a hat.) It is not fulfilling the purpose for which it was created.

Then explain the Christian belief that God created human beings to be in relationship with him, and this is made possible through Jesus Christ. Unless Jesus is at the centre of our lives, like the hand is at the centre of the glove, we too will not completely fulfil the purpose for which we were created.

TEACHING POINT: God created us to be in relationship with him.

BIBLE REFERENCES: John 1:3; Genesis 1:26–31.

APPLICATION: Although you could adapt this talk to be more about finding your purpose in life, its best impact is as an explanation of how a relationship with Christ gives us true fulfilment.

THE WATERPROOF NEWSPAPER

THEMES: Belief, faith.

INTRODUCTION: If you like the idea of passing off the illusion that you are a master magician, this without doubt is the illustration for you! With minimal rehearsal, and even less raw talent, you can create a few gasps by making a glass of water disappear into a newspaper. If you're as magically inept as I am, you'll even shock yourself when it actually works!

The point of the illustration is that by first making a mess of the trick you persuade a brave volunteer to put themselves in the line of fire to display they have not just belief in you, but faith. The very visual nature of the illustration will give you an opportunity to make your point in a way that will be remembered.

YOU WILL NEED
- a couple of broadsheet newspapers
- a rigged newspaper (available from good magic suppliers for a few pounds)
- water
- waterproof bonnet
- cloth

OUTLINE: As an introduction, explain to the assembly that you would like to perform a trick that though impressive is quite difficult. As you say this, take a page from a large newspaper and fold it four times, creating a pocket. Using a few comic flourishes, take the water and pour into the real newspaper, telling the assembly how you will make it magically disappear. Once there is half a glass of water in the paper, dramatically open it up, resulting in water pouring all over the floor! Feigning embarrassment, apologise to the teachers and clean up with a cloth. To a degree, the illustration hits or flops on how well you set this section up.

Try to gain some sympathy from the assembly, asking for another chance and some verbal encouragement. Ask them, 'Who believes I can do it the second time around?' Hopefully you'll get a reasonable response, at which point you thank those who state belief in you.

Explain that for the second attempt you want to use a volunteer from those who said they believed in you. They will sit on a chair while you do the trick behind them, holding the newspaper over their head! The nature of school-work means you'll probably get dozens of volunteers or none at all. If you can't get one, use your skills to coax a victim onto the stage.

Once you have sat the volunteer down, get them to introduce themselves, and if there is time, have a bit of fun. Put the waterproof bonnet on them, explaining that it's to protect their hair. This always gets a laugh.

Then proceed with the trick. This time used the rigged newspaper from the magic supplier, and following the simple instructions thrill your audience with the success of the trick. Present your relieved volunteer with a prize and encourage some applause as they return to their seat.

For your link, talk about how people are often keen to say they believe something, but they never actually show faith and willingly prove it. You can use various examples of things we say we believe in, such as the victory of England football team, nice weather, good causes, God. As in this illustration, we say we believe, but when push comes to shove we are not prepared to put ourselves on the line. Many will say they believe the trick will work second time around, but fewer are actually prepared to volunteer and sit in the firing line to display their faith.

That is the difference between belief and faith. Many people say they believe in God, or words to that effect, but it counts for little or nothing, because what is important is proving it by putting ourselves on the line and showing faith.

TEACHING POINT: Many believe, but fewer have faith.

BIBLE REFERENCE: John 12:42–43.

APPLICATION: The talk will clearly be about faith in God, but there is some flexibility in how you make the point.

FILTHY RAGS

THEMES: Good deeds, heaven and hell.

INTRODUCTION: In this assembly, a man appears on stage, apparently giving an account of his life to God. At first he appears confident, but slowly things start to go wrong.

As with any other monologue, only a confident performer should attempt this piece. Although one of my favourite forms of drama, the monologue is not usually suited to assemblies, but I've used this one a fair few times and it gets a good response.

It probably works best if you are also doing classes in school during the day so students can ask you about its hard-hitting message.

YOU WILL NEED
- a briefcase
- a pile of filthy rags

SCRIPT: (PETER *is sitting on a chair centre stage, briefcase on his lap.*)

VOICE: Number 3846214, Mr Peter Benevolence. Time to give your account please. Thank you.

PETER: (*Confidently steps forward.*) Ah, hello. Do you mind if I . . .? (*Indicates putting briefcase down, which he does.*) Thank you. So this is where I find out if I take the up or down escalator, is it? . . . Yes, well I understand it's an account you want. It's difficult to know where to start really. You know, it's amazing how you always wonder and worry about suffering some horrific death in a spectacular accident or from some life-draining disease. Well, nothing could have ever prepared me for my untimely demise. Picture the scene: I'm walking to work—a delicious packed lunch of Spam sandwiches safely stowed in the briefcase—when all of a sudden, without any word of warning, WHACK! A great big chimney pot falls on top of my head. Well, there was blood and gore all over the shop, and the next thing I know, here I am. Totally unbelievable, isn't it? You probably don't believe me . . . oh, what am I talking about? Of course you believe me. You probably planned it all anyway . . . Yes . . .

Anyway, back to my account. I had planned ahead in anticipation of a scenario such as this, so I've got everything possibly relevant recorded, logged and filed in my trusty briefcase. For starters, I've been a regular churchgoer all my life. Every Christmas, every Easter and a mass of weddings, funerals, christenings etceteras, etceteras, and on each occasion I've made a very generous donation to the church funds—of the rustling, not rattling, kind if you get my drift. Anyway, all this has been logged and receipted in the little black cashbook, which you'll find in the trusty briefcase. In addition to this, I have records of my long and prolific history of generous and regular giving to charity. I'll name a few of the beneficiaries. There's been the RSPCA, RSPB, RNLI, NCH, NSPCC, ACET, ABC, XYZ and the BFG. (*Looks confused.*) Anyway, all these records can be found logged in the dark green accounts book, again in the trusty briefcase. What else can I tell you about? . . . Ooh yes. Good deeds. How could I forget? Money doesn't solve everything. Well, to be honest I've done it all, from charity jumble sales to helping old dears across the street. Everyone always knew, if there's anything you need any help with you can always rely on trustworthy Peter Benevolence to give you a helping hand. Now all this information and more can be found in the navy blue file entitled 'Good works', which you'll also find in the trusty briefcase.

Well, how am I doing? I think I've got everything covered. What more can I say? I've been a nice guy, good to my family and friends. On the religious side of things I suppose I've never been the fanatical type, but I don't necessarily see that as a bad thing, do you? I mean, just think of all the wars that have kicked off in the name of religion . . . Not to say that's your fault, of course, but the point I'm making is . . . well, my faith's always been a very personal thing really, just between me and . . . well, me and me I suppose! I've always believed in you, sort of, ish, although I must admit it's quite overwhelming to meet you face to face like this. (*Short pause, awaiting response*.) Well, say something then. Aren't you going to say anything? . . . No . . . It's not going too well, is it? . . . Well, what else can I say? If you don't believe me look in the case, please. (*Loses temper*.) Oh just look in the case, for God's . . . (*Stops himself, calms down*.) Please, just look in the case. (*He picks up case and it flips open, spilling a pile of filthy rags and a message, which he reads*.) All of us have become like one who is unclean and all our righteous acts are like filthy rags. We all shrivel up like a leaf, and like the wind our sins sweep us away. (*Pause*.) Father, don't you remember me? (*Pause, look of fear*.) So which escalator is it to be then? Up or . . . up or down? (*Pause*.) Thank you, thank you. (*He picks up briefcase, takes a deep breath and exits*.)

TEACHING POINT: It is possible to do good things but have wrong motives or become self-righteous.

BIBLE REFERENCE: Matthew 7:21–23.

APPLICATION: Good deeds and a religious appearance are no substitute for a personal relationship with Jesus.

MUMMY RISES

THEMES: Resurrection, Easter.

INTRODUCTION: This illustration may not be the most original in the world (I think it probably appears at most children's parties), but it is great fun and has a very visual way of making a point. The very appearance of toilet rolls has an impact on our most base comic tastes, and wrapping up a couple of pupils in reams of the stuff has obvious appeal!

By setting up a competition (boys versus girls is most popular) you will gain attention and have a platform to speak on issues surrounding death and resurrection.

With the youngest pupils, be careful how graphic you make your visuals and descriptions of the crucifixion.

YOU WILL NEED
- sufficient toilet rolls to make two mummies

OUTLINE: Introduce the assembly by saying how interesting it is that the world is obsessed with death, or more specifically life after death. People often pretend they are not concerned, but in most cases they are. Even the cinema complexes are full of films on that theme: *The Others, Sixth Sense, Return of the Living Dead* and the *Mummy* films.

Ask the students to consider what they believe about life after death, then ask for some volunteers: three boys and three girls. Explain that one of each sex will be made into a mummy by the other two. In advance choose a judge (yourself, a colleague or teacher) and say that the winning team will receive a chocolate bar each. Give the exercise a time limit (a couple of minutes is about right), then ask the rest of the assembly to cheer for their respective team.

When time is up, try and have some fun with the volunteers—at least one is usually a complete disaster! Crown the champions and award the prizes.

Link back to your opening thought, suggesting that the mummies made today would struggle to last five minutes, let alone a thousand years!

Suggest that when people think of someone dying then coming back to life, the most obvious example is probably Jesus. But many people have said that although they believe in Jesus they're not so sure he actually died. This is a fair point and the most obvious thing to question, so you're going to check out what would happen to a body during and after a crucifixion in the case of Jesus. (If you can support these facts and evidences with visuals that would be an advantage, though not totally necessary.)

• He would have been brutally beaten.
• He would have been nailed to a cross for six hours, through his wrists and feet.
• He would have had a spear thrust in his side to check he was dead before being removed from the cross.
• He would have been wrapped in yards of cloth and soaked in heavy spices.
• He would have been left in a cold, airless tomb for at least 36 hours.

It takes a lot of faith to believe anyone can survive that! So assuming he really did die, was that the end of the story, or is there more we need to know about Jesus?

Close by saying that as Christians we believe so, and that it has great importance. If doing lessons during the day, explain that you will add to some of these thoughts later in the day.

TEACHING POINT: Jesus really died! How should we respond?

BIBLE REFERENCE: Luke 24:1–12.

APPLICATION: A thought-provoking challenge regarding the death of Jesus.

CALENDAR SYSTEM

THEMES: Jesus, Christianity, history.

INTRODUCTION: In this sketch two friends debate the relevance and existence of Jesus. Kate introduces an interesting argument that the calendar system revolves around Jesus' life on earth—strong evidence indeed for his significance on the world stage.

This piece can effectively stand alone or, using its themes, be built on during any subsequent lessons.

YOU WILL NEED
- a Bible
- a diary

SCRIPT: This sketch has been written for a man and a woman, but can easily be adapted.

(KATE *is sitting centre stage reading a Bible.* BRIAN *enters.*)

BRIAN: Oh no—do me a favour! You're not reading that Bible again.

KATE: (*Looks at cover.*) Apparently so . . .

BRIAN: I don't know why you bother. You might just as well read a book of nursery rhymes for all the truth you're gonna find in there.

KATE: (*Sarcastically.*) Well excuse me, Mr theological genius!

BRIAN: Look, I don't claim to have read it, but come on! Jesus Christ, Son of God—it's pathetic. Even if he did exist as some kind of bearded, sandalled nomad 2,000 years ago, that hardly affects us today.

KATE: You really believe that? That Jesus Christ has no relevance at all?

BRIAN: Not a jot.

KATE: (*Pause.*) Have you got your diary on you?

BRIAN: (*Confused.*) My diary? Yeah, 'course. (*Gets out diary.*)

KATE: (*Points.*) What does that say?

BRIAN: Ooh yeah, lunch at 12.30 with Sandra from the newsagent's!

KATE: No, not that. There!

BRIAN: What? The date? June 2003.

KATE: (*In deep thought.*) Yeah, 2003. World's young, innit?

BRIAN: Well, it's been going for a bit longer than that.

KATE: Do you think? How much longer?

BRIAN: Well I don't know! What is this? A history lesson? Must be a few hundred thousand years or something—probably more.

KATE: So why does it only say 2003 there then?

BRIAN: That's obviously when they started the calendar system, isn't it?

KATE: So how can we date something that happened over 2,000 years ago then?

BRIAN: Are you thick? Dates are now carried forward with the letters AD, and anything earlier is counted in reverse followed by the letters BC. Didn't they teach you anything at school?

KATE: All right, clever clogs. What do BC and AD stand for?

BRIAN: Before Christ and . . . (*Tails off, realising he's been caught out.*)

KATE: (*Sarcastically.*) Pardon? I didn't catch that. Did you say 'Before Christ'? Let me get this straight. You think the world's calendar system is centred on a totally irrelevant man who possibly didn't exist. Seems a bit unlikely doesn't it?

BRIAN: All right, all right, you've made your point!

KATE: (*Having fun.*) I mean, you'd think they could have found someone a bit better to bestow this honour on—Julius Caesar, Cleopatra, David Beckham! Hey, that's not a bad idea. Maybe we can start a new calendar system around him. (BRIAN *slowly exits.*) Before David Beckham: BDB. After the birth of Romeo: ABR. What do you think of that, Brian? . . . Brian?

TEACHING POINT: Jesus Christ is the pivotal figure in human history.

BIBLE REFERENCE: Hebrews 13:8.

APPLICATION: Although not overtly evangelistic in its content, the sketch has a clear message about the importance of Christ.

BUS STOP

THEMES: Lifestyle, stillness, listening.

INTRODUCTION: This idea centres around an exercise commonly used in drama or theatre-based workshops. I've used it many times and as well as being very entertaining, it does make a good point that can easily be linked into your theme.

Basically, a couple of volunteers are asked to act out standing at a bus stop. The results are often unpredictable, but usually very funny. Regardless of what the volunteers come up with, you can easily link into the point that in life we are so busy that we sometimes need to just stop and listen.

OUTLINE: To open the assembly do a quick straw poll among the students on how people got to school this morning. Did they walk, cycle, get a lift, catch a bus or skateboard? End by making the point that buses are a very useful mode of transport, but can so often cause frustration by running late.

Now ask for two volunteers who are willing to do a little bit of acting. Once you have chosen them, they both need to be taken out of earshot by a third person while you explain to the rest of the assembly what will happen next.

Each volunteer has the task of acting out waiting at a bus stop for a period of 60 seconds. During that time the bus does not arrive, nor do any other passengers. They're on their own. There's not even a seat or shelter—just a basic bus stop with a timetable on the post. Ask for a few suggestions as to what they might do.

While you explain that to the assembly, the third person gives the two volunteers exactly the same instructions. Impress on them that there is no catch and no exclusively correct way of doing it. They should just go with what they think seems right.

One at a time the volunteers come up to perform (the second should not see the first). You should time them for a minute, which will seem like a very long time. Be prepared for anything in these performances. Sometimes you'll get an embarrassed shambles; other times there will be wild gesticulation, watch tapping, constant tutting and searching for the bus, reading a paper, playing a Walkman, etc.

Once the time is up ask them how they felt, and if in retrospect they think it was an accurate portrayal of waiting at a bus stop. Also ask for a couple of other comments from the floor: what people liked, what they thought should have been done differently. Whatever is said, ensure you praise the volunteers at the end for being brave enough to do what is in fact a very difficult task. Award prizes and initiate some applause.

The point you are working towards is that the actions always tend to be too busy, and full of exaggerated movement. In reality, if you were on your own at a bus stop for a few minutes, you would probably hardly move. You'd just stand there, maybe glance at your watch, but basically you'd do nothing.

Link this to how we humans find it so difficult to keep still and do nothing. (Standing motionless in front of an audience for a whole minute is much more difficult than it sounds.) At this point I tell a story about my nephew on a car trip, constantly fidgeting and asking 'Are we nearly there yet?'

Then go on to say that in our frantic society where it's so hard to find peace—where people are constantly watching television, sending texts, playing music, playing computer games and talking on the telephone (often all at the same time!)—we need sometimes to be still.

Further link this to a spiritual point by saying that in the Bible we read the words, 'Be still and know that I am God.' Yes, by all means we can enjoy a variety of loud, full-on hobbies—we don't need to be peaceful 24/7 as if we were in some kind of retreat—but we need to create some time and space to be quiet and listen, to take in. If we don't, we could miss out.

TEACHING POINT: The importance of finding peace and stillness in a restless world.

BIBLE REFERENCE: Psalm 46:10.

APPLICATION: If appropriate, you could end by giving a personal testimony of how you take a quiet time out, and the benefit you get from it.

THE WHY FILES

THEMES: Easter, resurrection.

INTRODUCTION: Predictably from the title, this piece is loosely based on the BBC TV series, *The X Files*. Sulker and Mouldy are paranormal experts working for Pontius Pilate, discussing the mystery surrounding the resurrection. Using music and costume relating to the programme will certainly add to the sketch. With a couple of tweaks both roles can be played by a male or female.

The aim is to provide the very basics of the Easter story in a nutshell, and the themes raised can be built on creatively if there are opportunities to lead any lessons.

YOU WILL NEED
- suitable costumes
- two torches
- a Why file prop
- backdrop of an empty tomb (optional)

SCRIPT: (SULKER *and* MOULDY *enter, shining torches. There is creepy* X Files *music playing. Suddenly one torch beam dies.*)

SULKER: Oh, typical!

MOULDY: What's up?

SULKER: The batteries have gone on my flippin' torch.

MOULDY: I told you to buy Duracells, didn't I?

SULKER: Oh shut up!

MOULDY: But oh no, you had to get the cheap ones from Woolies!

SULKER: Shut up, will you! Anyway, it's probably only a loose connection. (*Shakes and bangs torch; beam returns.*) Aha—see! What did I tell you?

MOULDY: Good, I'm so pleased for you. Now shine it over here so I can read this file.

SULKER: Is it an X file?

MOULDY: No, it's a Why file.

SULKER: A Why file?

MOULDY: Yes. Apparently Governor Pilate has got a bit of a problem with a mysterious empty tomb. So he's called in his crack team of highly trained paranormal operatives to find out why.

SULKER: Ooh! Highly trained paranormal experts. Who are they?

MOULDY: Us!

SULKER: Us? Oh no! Why do we always get lumbered with the manky jobs?

MOULDY: Oh, stop sulking, Agent Sulker. This is a good case.

SULKER: Come on then, give us the background.

MOULDY: That's more like it. (*Reads from file.*) Well, this guy Jesus, after a spell of preaching, teaching, performing miracles and claiming to be the Son of God, got himself in a bit of bother with the religious authorities, who, to cut a long story short, sentenced him to death.

SULKER: Yeah, skip all that—I read about it in the *Jerusalem Herald*.

MOULDY: Well, after he died, he was buried in the tomb right behind us. Three days later, we have one missing corpse, one empty tomb and one extremely panicky governor.

SULKER: Ppff! They called us in for a simple one like that?

MOULDY: Hang on, there's one more thing. Since the disappearance of the body, there have been dozens of sightings of Jesus around town, apparently looking in tiptop condition.

SULKER: (*Pause.*) Ah, well that puts a slightly different complexion on things. But come on, Agent Mouldy, think rationally. Before we consider the paranormal, we need to eliminate the normal. There are loads of possible explanations.

MOULDY: Come on then. I'm all ears.

SULKER: Well, for a start, how do we know Jesus actually died?

MOULDY: Are you being serious?

SULKER: Every avenue should be explored, wouldn't you agree?

MOULDY: Yes, yes I agree. We should examine this avenue most carefully. Well, for a start he was flogged within an inch of his life. He was then nailed to a cross through his wrists and feet and left for six hours, and just for good measure he had a spear shoved in his side . . .

SULKER: I see your point . . .

MOULDY: Hang on, there's more. If you still think he could have survived that little lot, he then would have had to last out in a non-air-conditioned tomb without any water for a couple of days, remove layers of cloth soaked in gallons of spices, and then, for his absolute *pièce de résistance*, shove away a ten tonne stone.

SULKER: Mmm, so basically what you're saying is . . .

MOULDY: What I'm saying is, I think we can safely assume he died.

SULKER: Then he must have been removed.

MOULDY: Who by? David Blaine the magician?

SULKER: Don't be daft! Removed as in stolen.

MOULDY: Stolen? Well, I've heard of people nicking car stereos and video recorders, but who would want to steal a dead body?

SULKER: His disciples.

MOULDY: How did they manage that then, with a couple of burly security guards on 24-hour watch?

SULKER: Well, I don't know. Maybe they arranged some kind of distraction. A couple of dolly birds with low-cut tops and ra-ra skirts.

MOULDY: Ra-ra skirts!

SULKER: You know what I mean. They distract the burly security guards, his disciples come in from the other side, push away the stone and make off with the corpse.

MOULDY: Brilliant! Governor Pilate is currently concocting all manner of horrible deaths for his disciples, and they'd be willing to die knowing it was all some cock and bull story. I don't think so.

SULKER: Oh, you're always so negative.

MOULDY: That's 'cos all your ideas suck!

SULKER: Aha! I think I've got it!

MOULDY: Here we go again.

SULKER: A government cover up.

MOULDY: Oh no, here goes Miss Paranoid.

SULKER: Come on, Mouldy, you know what these government officials can be like. Yes, I bet they removed him to undertake some highly confidential experiments, or for political gain in the run up to the next election.

MOULDY: Hardly likely, is it, birdbrain?

SULKER: Why not?

MOULDY: If Governor Pilate is running around like a headless chicken trying to get answers, it's hardly likely he's nicked the body himself, is it? If he had it, he'd produce it sharpish to put an end to all the unrest and rumours.

SULKER: All right, clever clogs. So let's recap. We know Jesus definitely died and was put in the tomb under round-the-clock guard. The disciples couldn't have stolen him, and even if they could have, they wouldn't martyr themselves for some fairy story. And the government can't have anything to do with it or they would have spoken up and nipped the rumours in the bud.

MOULDY: Precisely.

SULKER: So, Agent Mouldy, where exactly does that leave us?

MOULDY: In all honesty, I haven't got a clue. But I'll tell you what. The truth is out there.

SULKER: You're right about that. Somewhere, the truth is out there.

TEACHING POINT: The Easter evidence points towards a resurrection miracle.

BIBLE REFERENCE: Mark 16:1–8.

APPLICATION: The use of drama should make the overt message more easily digestible.

THEY THINK IT'S ALL OVER

THEME: Relevance of Jesus.

INTRODUCTION: I'm sure most people have seen the BBC sports panel game *They Think It's All Over*. Probably the most popular, or at least most memorable, round is where the teams are blind-folded and have to guess the celebrity by touch alone.

This assembly uses this basic idea to make a surprising point about the relevance of Jesus today, 2,000 years after his earthly life.

YOU WILL NEED
- costumes as described
- blindfolds
- prizes

OUTLINE: Before the assembly, if you haven't already, watch an episode of *They Think It's All Over* to familiarise yourself with the game.

To begin, ask for a show of hands of those who have seen the show *They Think It's All Over*. Ask what they think of the show, who's the funniest contestant, which is the best round, etc. Make a few observations of your own, saying that your favourite round is the mystery guest.

Now ask for four volunteers to be panellists in your own mini version of the game live on stage. Split them into two teams of two, and blindfold the first team.

Next invite your first sporting celebrity onto the stage. This is a member of your party dressed up in a suitable costume. You can stretch the rules by not limiting yourself to sports stars. The key is to choose very famous but very old stars that the kids will never have heard of! A few examples would be W. G. Grace, Glenn Miller and Humphrey Bogart. Think of your own that were genuinely superstars and give an excuse for a funny costume. (W. G. Grace in whites and a long beard is a real winner!)

Run the first round like this, feigning shock and apologies when the students inevitably claim they've never heard of the stars.

For the second round, use really obvious up-to-date celebrities the kids will definitely guess (feel free to give a few clues, and encourage the other students to do so). Court some applause for the volunteers and award a small prize to the winners.

Link this illustration to the thought of how much difference a few years make. Everyone knew the current stars, but they'd never heard of the old ones. Just 50 or 60 years back, though, they were the David Beckhams and Robbie Williamses of their day! W. G. Grace was a hugely famous cricketer, Bogart was number one at the box office and Glenn Miller had all their grandparents dancing in the dance halls! (These can be interchanged with anyone you choose.)

Further link this to the fact that Jesus lived over 2,000 years ago—pre computers, electricity, cars and even Bic biros! Yet some claim that he was and is completely irrelevant. Just a carpenter. Just a do-gooder. Basically a nobody! In 100 years, possibly even just 50, hardly anyone will have a clue who David

Beckham or Robbie Williams was, even though at present they are so famous. Do you really think it is possible that Jesus would still be so widely known today if he was just an irrelevant nobody?

TEACHING POINT: Discovering the relevance of Jesus today.

BIBLE REFERENCE: Hebrews 13:8.

APPLICATION: A fun illustration, ending with a Christian thought-provoker.

MY HOPE IS IN JAMES BOND

KS2 KS3 KS4

THEME: Hope.

INTRODUCTION: I like using this illustration because I really am a fully signed-up James Bond fan! If you're not a fan you can still do this one, but you'll have to pretend a little bit!

The point of the assembly is to give a Christian view of hope, being something that is sure and certain, compared to the other kind of hope, which is a bit more hit and miss.

YOU WILL NEED
- various props (choose your own, but suggestions include rope, clip-on bow tie, cuddly cat, Russian hat, something resembling a man-eating shark! In short, be creative)

OUTLINE: Walk on stage to a quick blast of the James Bond theme. Open by asking the assembly if they recognise the theme. Go on to tell them what a fan you are and ask if there are any other fans in the assembly. If there has been a Bond film at the cinema recently, ask who has been to see it. If you have time, do a quick vote on who the most popular Bond is. If possible, accompany this with pictures. It will probably end up with a victory for Pierce Brosnan and a joke at the expense of George Lazenby!

Now explain that your favourite part of the movies is when Bond inevitably gets himself into a seemingly hopeless mess. He's tied up upside down, dangling over man-eating sharks, powerful laser beam aimed at him . . . In human terms the situation is hopeless.

Now say that to help them get this image in mind you're going to re-create a Bond movie live, for which you will need two volunteers: Bond and the archetypal villain.

Once you have your volunteers, have some fun with a bag of props. Maybe Bond is tied up, still looking dapper in his bow tie with killer sharks at his feet? The villain could be stroking a cat, wearing a Russian hat. The possibilities are endless, but the more creative and funny the better.

Ask the volunteers to act out a short scene. Have the words printed on cards. I suggest something very simple like:

BOND: The name's Bond, James Bond.
VILLAIN: Ah, we've been expecting you, Mr Bond!
BOND: And I suppose you expect me to talk, you villainous scum?
VILLAIN: No, Mr Bond. I expect you to die! (*Evil laugh*.)

Depending on the confidence of the two volunteers, get them to perform it a couple of times, encouraging them to really go for it.

Now ask the assembly: Who thinks that despite his position Bond will survive? (The response should be that he will.) Further quiz them, pointing out that the odds don't look good. He's pretty strapped up and things look hopeless. (Maybe at this point ask your brave volunteers what they think would happen.) Then ask them to sit down, and elicit some enthusiastic applause for them.

Link this to the message, saying that although we can see Bond is in trouble we know he will survive because he always does in every movie. We can put our hope in him because we know the end of the movie. Similarly when Christians speak of the hope they have in Christ, it's not a wishy-washy hope like 'I hope it doesn't rain tomorrow' or 'I hope Brighton and Hove Albion win the league'. It is a hope that is certain.

TEACHING POINT: The sure and certain hope offered through Jesus.

BIBLE REFERENCE: Ephesians 2:12–13.

APPLICATION: Christians believe that Jesus Christ gives true hope. Through him we know the end of the movie.

IT'S A KIND OF MAGIC

THEMES: Magic, miracles.

INTRODUCTION: It can be difficult to talk about miracles at the best of times, because by their very nature they tend to be pretty unbelievable (which is of course what makes them miraculous). Using the trusted old device of a magic trick we can introduce the theme of miracles and hopefully have the assembly questioning whether they believe in anything that is supernatural.

For those who are unable to perform any tricks, don't panic. I've given an alternative that is equally effective and requires absolutely no magical prowess!

YOU WILL NEED
• props for your trick, as described

OUTLINE: Begin the assembly by performing a trick—anything that is fun and visual, and preferably involves using a volunteer. If you are unable to do any tricks, here are two alternative routes that enable you to make the same point.

1. If you have prior contact with the school, pick a student to act as a stooge or plant in the assembly. The opportunities are then limitless for performing a trick that is basically a total cheat!
2. I have often used the method of setting up a really impressive trick that engages the assembly, but at the last minute it all goes wrong. For instance, claim you can make a randomly chosen card stick against a blackboard. Choose a volunteer, who selects a card, shows it to the assembly and signs it. Then they shuffle the pack and you announce that you are going to throw the pack against the blackboard and the card will stick. You really play the whole thing up, and then of course the trick fails miserably.

Depending on the method you use—real trick, student plant or disastrous trick—link this into comments on the types of magic we see. Are they genuine or hoaxes?

Quiz the students on what they think of the various magicians they see on the television. What do they make of card sharks? Clever sleight of hand, outrageous cheating or a trick of the camera? How about hypnotists? Genuine playing with the mind or pre-prepared acting? Finally, what about illusionists? What do they make of some of the amazing stunts by the likes of David Blaine? Does he truly possess magical powers, or is it all a hoax and we're being made fools of? What do they believe?

TEACHING POINT: The difference between magic and miracles.

BIBLE REFERENCE: John 2:23.

APPLICATION: Link to the point that the Bible is full of miracles: water into wine; feeding 5,000; walking on water. They are recorded not as sleight-of-hand tricks but as supernatural miracles. Of course they seem hard to believe, as they go against the natural order of things, but Christians believe that Jesus performed these miracles, as he was the Son of God and had supernatural powers. He was not governed by what we perceive as possible. For us, the question is: Do we believe this? Is there such a thing as supernatural power? Were these incidents in fact genuine miracles or some kind of deceptive magic?

THE STICKY PROBLEM OF SIN

THEMES: Sin, salvation, the gospel.

INTRODUCTION: This popular illustration could potentially be rather cheesy if an outside group came in to present it cold, but if you have links to a school and can arrange for some pupils to take part it can be great fun.

Using the idea of a man (and subsequently other characters) getting stuck on a chair, you get a visual image of the power of sin. From this you can link to a basic gospel message.

YOU WILL NEED
- a chair with a 'Do not touch' sign
- 4–6 volunteers, pre-prepared and rehearsed

OUTLINE: In advance, rehearse with a group of four to six pupils for the following mime illustration. Basically you have a chair centre stage with a 'Do not touch' sign. A person enters and walks by, and then, tempted by the sign, furtively looks around and touches the chair, only to get stuck. The more they try to escape, the worse it becomes, with more parts of the body getting stuck. Eventually they mime shouting for help. One by one the remaining volunteers come along and try to help, but they also get stuck and join in with the cries for help.

If this is well rehearsed it can look really funny: people stuck in awkward positions with amusing facial expressions. The illustration ends with all the group stuck, miming shouts for help. If you can, use a light fade or pull a curtain to end the illustration.

Having encouraged some applause for the volunteer actors, link your short talk to the illustration by picking up the 'Do not touch' sign and turning it over. On the reverse is the word 'SIN'.

First explain that the word 'sin' has been given a bad press as some soppy religious word, but basically it means the things we do wrong and know are wrong. Give an example, such as a thief or mugger knowing what they do is wrong. Whether they change their behaviour is a different thing, but like us all they have a built-in code that says they're doing wrong.

Further explain that Christians believe sin is what blocks us from a relationship with God, and Jesus is the way by which we can be reconciled. Word the message however you feel comfortable, including the following points:

- God created us and gave us free will.
- Mankind has chosen rebellion from day one and continues to do so.
- God, in his love, has given humans a second chance and this is provided through Jesus.
- If we turn to Jesus we are reconciled to God and will be for eternity.

TEACHING POINT: The forgiveness of sin through Jesus.

BIBLE REFERENCE: Romans 3:23–26.

APPLICATION: This is an overtly evangelistic gospel message. Remember: always refer to these truths as 'what Christians believe' or start with: 'As a Christian I believe . . .'

I'M WITH THE WOOLWICH

THEMES: Allegiance, belief.

INTRODUCTION: One of the most common misconceptions about Christianity (and therefore well worth covering in an assembly) is the belief that because we're British, we're automatically Christian. In one sense it may seem a rather obvious point to make, but communicating the fact that Christianity is a free-will choice made by an individual rather than an automatic right is very important.

YOU WILL NEED
• various visual props as described, but creatively use your own

OUTLINE: Open with a story about an incorrect assumption regarding someone's allegiance. You can use the example of the man wearing a Brazil football tracksuit. You could assume he was from Brazil, until you hear him speak with a Cockney accent. Of course the truth is he just likes the team, or probably the colour and design of the top, and has likely never even been to Brazil in his life.

Ask for a show of hands of Manchester United fans. Find out how long people have been fans and how many own a team shirt or any other paraphernalia. Next find out how many have been to see a game at Old Trafford or even actually been to Manchester! There is a ridiculously large percentage of Manchester United fans who have never been to Manchester—even to England, for that matter. (By the way, this particular section of the illustration won't work in Manchester! Use another example of an incorrect assumption regarding allegiance such as someone having a signed photo of a famous pop group when they've never actually met the group.)

We make assumptions about people, and even ourselves, based on what we wear, things we say or do and even on where we come from. Explain that Great Britain is a Christian state—we have a Church of England and our monarch is a defender of the faith. Based on this, people incorrectly assume they are Christian. They have an allegiance based solely on the origin of their birth. They say, 'I must be Christian: I'm British!' or 'I must be a Christian: I was christened.' People automatically put Christianity for their religion on official forms at census time, on medical forms, documents, etc. Why?

Explain the Christian belief that faith is not an automatic thing, but a choice we each make individually. Yes, being British gives us ample opportunity to hear what the Bible has to say through the church, various teaching and by easy access to the Bible itself. But the question is: Do we believe it and act upon it? Are we prepared to consciously make that allegiance?

TEACHING POINT: Christian faith is a conscious choice, not an automatic right.

BIBLE REFERENCE: Joshua 24:15.

APPLICATION: What choices have you made in life? What decision have you made regarding your faith?

GOD'S MEGAPHONE

THEMES: Hearing God, pain.

INTRODUCTION: I love C. S. Lewis's famous description of pain as 'God's megaphone to rouse a deaf world'. (See *The Problem of Pain*, Collins 1940, p. 8.) In this assembly we use this very simple idea as the centrepiece of our illustration. In our Western culture, with all its affluence and mod cons, it's very easy to ignore God completely, taking for granted the creation all around us. Often it is in our times of despair and trouble, when some of the material crutches have been kicked away, that we find ourselves turning to God, and he is speaking to us through his megaphone.

YOU WILL NEED
- a megaphone (the P.E. department should have one)

OUTLINE: Open by sharing some of your humorous pet hates (anything will suffice—made up ones are allowed!). Mine include people who spot new car registration plates on the first day of issue, stupid signs (like 'This way to the end of the pier') and Celine Dion! End by saying that one of your biggest pet hates is people talking when you're talking or, even worse, talking in the cinema.

Now choose two volunteers, one to stand at the back and one to stand on the stage, for an experiment. You give the person on stage a basic phrase to say to the person at the back of the hall, such as, 'Can you direct me to the toilet please?' Ask the rest of the assembly to turn to their neighbour and mutter the word 'mutter' over and over. This is quite funny in itself and in a large hall will be surprisingly loud and should block out the effort of communication.

Once the assembly are muttering, direct the volunteer on stage to begin the challenge. The first time they whisper the message. (This should fail.) The second time they speak the message at normal volume. (This also should fail.) The third time they speak loudly through the megaphone. (This should work!)

After the volunteers are seated and order has been restored, link this to how often messages don't get through as intended. Sometimes we have to repeat a message, or even resort to shouting it in order to be heard. Sometimes the message is blocked because life is too busy with the general hubbub and things happening all around us.

TEACHING POINT: God can speak to us through our pain.

BIBLE REFERENCE: Psalm 29.

APPLICATION: Link to the message that Christians believe God desires to communicate with everyone on the planet. But if so, why are there so many people unaware of him, all refusing to acknowledge him? In our comfortable Western existence, with everything provided for us from fast pain relief to disposable contact lenses, life seems like a breeze and we feel very self-sufficient.

End by saying that the writer C. S. Lewis described pain as God's megaphone. That might seem odd or even cruel, but it is true that often in our times of most trouble, when creature comforts are of little help, we catch a glimpse of God.

INTO THE ARMS OF FAITH

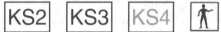

THEMES: Faith, trust.

INTRODUCTION: The illustration that forms the basis of this assembly has been used in just about every context imaginable simply because it's a real winner. I've included a couple of possible methods—one more familiar and the other maybe for the more daring (or possibly downright stupid!) among you. With both, the simple lesson is that we can give lip service to how we trust someone until we're blue in the face, but until we put it into action and exercise faith it means little or nothing.

Without wishing to sound melodramatic, it would be wise to note that this illustration involves a small degree of physical contact with the students. During preparation, practise how to catch a person with your arms straight, keeping physical contact to a minimum.

OUTLINE: Explain to the assembly that in the world there are some people we trust and others we do not. Get some student feedback on some of the following:

- Parents.
- Teachers. (If you have a good relationship with specific teachers pick them, but be careful not to undermine teachers, as it will inevitably backfire.)
- The prime minister.
- The pope.

The list is endless—add some of your own. End by asking if they trust you or if they think you trust them (depending on method used).

Method 1
Ask to the front a volunteer who claims to trust you. Challenge them to close their eyes and fall backwards—totally straight, no knee bending—and trust you to catch them. (Usually they won't refuse, but if they do, find a new volunteer.) You might need a couple of attempts at this because students may bend their knees, which displays a lack of trust, so they should have another go. Make sure you step back a bit so that they have to fall a fair way before you catch them. If you haven't done this before, practice with a friend beforehand is essential. Whatever happens, the point regarding trust and faith is made.

Method 2
If you are feeling brave you can reverse the whole thing and choose six volunteers to catch you! Get them to stand in two rows of three, arms locked, creating a kind of stretcher. You then take a long run up and dive into the students' locked arms! (One of my friends used this demonstration by standing on the edge of the stage and falling backwards into the students' arms. Not realising he was being serious, they dropped him!)

Whichever method you opt for, faith and trust are illustrated, giving you the platform for the message that, by literally putting your faith into other people's hands, you display true trust and faith.

TEACHING POINT: Faith is best displayed in action.

BIBLE REFERENCE: James 2:14–24.

APPLICATION: Link to the Christian belief that when people say they have faith in God, it should manifest itself in their actions.

SO NEAR, YET SO FAR

THEMES: Religions, truth.

INTRODUCTION: It is true to say that there are degrees of error. You can answer a question and be totally off the mark, or you can be tantalisingly close—so near, yet so far.

In this assembly we attempt to look briefly at the question of other religions. Many people's doubts about any religion spring from the fact that they are all so exclusive, claiming to have the only way, the unarguable truth. Of course there has to be a truth, but with so many 'truths' vying for attention, how do we know which one to choose?

YOU WILL NEED
• a flip chart or OHP with prewritten questions

OUTLINE: Explain to the assembly that you are going to ask them a few questions to attempt to find out the difference between right and wrong. The three rounds will be maths, English and science.

For the maths round, put a multiplication question up on the OHP. Don't make it too easy, but it should be one they can do in their heads, e.g. 8×13. Ask a volunteer to answer and go on until you get the correct response. Tell them that 104 is the correct answer, going on to say that 103.99 is very close, 107 is pretty close and 2,642 is vaguely ridiculous.

For the next two rounds follow a similar pattern. In the English round choose a spelling, e.g. suspicious. Again, get volunteers to answer until one gets it right, further explaining that 'suspicouis' is close, 'sushpisious' is understandable, but 'sxxifghlems' is a bit daft! In the science round you could ask for the chemical formula that represents a given substance, making the point that to get just one symbol wrong could make the difference between a safe substance and a lethal one. But of course these are only examples. Feel free to choose your own.

Draw from the illustration the point that however near to the truth any of the incorrect answers were, they were still wrong and in an exam setting would have earned an equal nil points.

Then go on to say that one of people's biggest problems with any of the major religions is that they all claim to be the only truth—the one and only route to God—and that everyone else is wrong. Christians believe that Jesus Christ is the only route to God, as revealed in the Bible. It may seem arrogant for Christians or any other religion to claim that they are the only ones to have it right, but by its definition there has to be a truth. Briefly explain these typical arguments with illustrations:

- 'All roads lead to God.' But if you study the different religions they often run contrary to one another, making this argument impossible.
- 'Most religions are pretty close anyway.' Some religions share much of the teaching of Christianity, but as in our earlier examples however close you are to the truth you can still be totally wrong.
- 'Surely if you're sincere in what you believe, that is enough.' But simply having sincerity is not enough. Hitler may have been sincere in his plan to purge the world of millions of Jews, but he was wrong. I may be sincere in my belief that

Brighton and Hove Albion are the best football team in the world, but I might be wrong.

Tie up by saying that Christianity is unique in the claims it makes. As individuals we must decide whether we believe it to be the truth.

TEACHING POINT: Is Christianity the only way to God?

BIBLE REFERENCE: John 14:6.

APPLICATION: A thought-provoking challenge about Christianity and other religions. It is important to discuss what you are planning to do with the head teacher responsible to avoid any possible misunderstanding, particularly in multiracial settings. Do not attempt this assembly until you have first built up a good relationship with the school and earned their trust and respect. If in doubt, leave it out!

CROSS PURPOSES

THEMES: The cross, salvation.

INTRODUCTION: A friend of mine once spotted the front page of a popular tabloid given over to the image of the cross of St George's flag, with words something like, 'This page is cancelled. Nothing else matters.' The event was of course England's ill-fated World Cup match with Brazil.

This tabloid headline gave rise to the idea of a slight slant on the illustration using the different meanings of the cross. This fun, participatory exercise gives the platform for teaching on the Christian view of the importance of the cross.

YOU WILL NEED
• quality visual aids depicting the various crosses

OUTLINE: Open by saying how strange it is that in different places or in different times things can have totally different meanings. Use a variety of examples such as:

- In America, if you ask for a bag of chips, you'll get a packet of crisps.
- Stateside still, your pants are actually your trousers.
- A few years ago the word 'gay' meant happy and friendly. Now it's a common term for a homosexual.
- When talking about the greatest football team in Liverpool, one part of the city will assume you mean the blues, whereas the other side will think red!

Link this to the huge number of meanings there are for the symbol of the cross. Display a simple picture of a cross, and then ask for some ideas of what it could mean. After these have died down, show some pre-prepared acetates or a Power Point presentation giving a variety of examples. They can include:

- An incorrect answer.
- A kiss at the bottom of a letter.
- A mark on a voting slip.
- A multiplication sign.
- An addition sign.
- A Roman numeral.
- The Christian cross.
- The St George's flag.

Go on to say that people place different importance on these things, but it is essential to know which one is meant, to avoid possible confusion. Next tell the story of the front page of the tabloid on the England and Brazil match mentioned in the introduction. Display an image of the flag with the words 'This page is cancelled. Nothing else matters'. Explain that however key that match was to the majority of the British public, to say that nothing else matters seems rather an exaggeration when there is conflict and famine in the world.

Central to what a Christian believes is the importance of the cross and what Jesus achieved when he died over 2,000 years ago. (Change the acetate to the Christian cross.) End the assembly by changing the words of the headline to 'Our sins are cancelled. Nothing else matters'.

TEACHING POINT: The importance of the cross.

BIBLE REFERENCE: John 3:16.

APPLICATION: This talk can be coupled with a very brief gospel thought or word of testimony.

THE POWERFUL PRINCE AND THE PRETTY PEASANT GIRL

THEMES: Freedom, love.

INTRODUCTION: People often argue that if God is so powerful, why doesn't he just make us love him and have done with it? Of course we don't really know for certain, but it probably has to do with the strange paradox of God's desire for us to love him but by our own free choice. Surely if he makes us love him, it takes away any meaning the gesture would have.

To illustrate this, we use the tale of the powerful prince and the pretty peasant girl, dramatising it with the help of two students. This should get a good laugh and make a clear point.

YOU WILL NEED
- a powerful prince costume
- a pretty peasant girl costume
- a keyboard (optional)

OUTLINE: Open the assembly by explaining that you are going to tell a fairy story and you need the help of one boy and one girl. Choose your volunteers, and if possible have somewhere out of sight where they can put on costumes, and have a helper to assist them. Be as creative as possible with the costumes.

Basically, you narrate the script (feel free to adapt mine) and coax the volunteers to act along, giving them a couple of bits of dialogue. If you can, have someone play some suitable background keyboard music to add dramatic and comic effect.

The tale of the powerful prince and the pretty peasant girl
Once upon a time, many many moons ago, there was a very pretty but extremely poor peasant girl. (GIRL *enters*.) She spent long hard days tending her vegetable garden and when she found a spare moment she enjoyed nothing more than dancing. While she worked and played in blissful solitude, far away a powerful and extremely rich prince looked on in awe. (BOY *appears from behind curtain*.) Yes, he had fallen deeply in love with the girl.

At night he couldn't sleep, thinking of the girl's beauty, and when he did drop off, minutes later he would wake up with a start, screaming, 'My pretty peasant girl!' (BOY *does this*.) One day he decided to do something about it. He would approach her. He reckoned that if he went in all his princely robes she would fall at his feet, impressed by his power, good looks and manly strength, and they would live happily ever after. But then he had second thoughts. If he showed his wealth, how would he know she truly loved him for who he was and didn't just want to get her mitts on all his worldly treasures? Suddenly inspiration struck. He would level the playing field. If he became a peasant too, and she still loved him, he would truly know she was genuine in her love. So he whipped his kit off, dressed up as a poor peasant and bravely approached her. (*Love music plays*.)

As their eyes met, they smiled, they swooned and they grasped hold of each other's hands. 'Hello, fair maiden,' said the prince. 'Greetings, weary traveller,' the peasant girl replied. (*They both speak their lines*.)

And did it all end happily ever after? Well, friends, that is for you to decide.

Encourage huge applause for the two brave actors, then link this story to teaching on free will. Ask the students whether they think the prince was wise in his approach to the girl. Should he have used the fact that he was rich and powerful to help make the girl fall for him? In the short term it may have made things easier, but in the long term he would never have been sure she'd loved him just for himself. She may have loved him out of obligation or for what she could gain.

Link this to how so often celebrity relationships go wrong. If someone is very famous, how can they be sure that romantic partners or friends are genuine and not just jumping on the celebrity bandwagon? Use some examples of current celebrity relationship disasters that may fit this pattern.

TEACHING POINT: How do we respond to the freedom given by God?

BIBLE REFERENCE: Galatians 5:1.

APPLICATION: Further link this to Christian teaching. People often question why God doesn't just make people love and follow him. Christians believe that God has given us the freedom to choose whether we follow him or not. He doesn't force us because if he did it would be meaningless, like the story of the prince and the peasant girl. Christians believe that God has taken the risk to give us freedom, and our challenge is how we respond to that freedom.

THE JESUS QUESTION

THEMES: Jesus, the Bible.

INTRODUCTION: I think one of the best ways to convince people that they're not as clued up on a topic as they think they are is to show them how little in fact they do know. This certainly applies to the Jesus question.

Competitions always work well in assemblies and certainly hold the attention, so a Jesus quiz, pitting the boys against the girls, will work well and hopefully make a good point.

This idea has certainly been well tried and tested over a number of years. I've used similar quizzes to this one on countless occasions, as have many other individuals and organisations.

YOU WILL NEED
- questions on acetate (optional)
- a creative score board

OUTLINE: Open by explaining to the students that you regularly take assemblies, often relating to Christian teaching, and the mere mention of the word 'Jesus' gets an interesting and immediate response:

- Some groan.
- Some are positive, because they believe in him.
- Some are surprised because they have only ever used the word to swear.
- Some feign indifference.
- Some are strongly anti.

Most people, however, do have some kind of opinion, but for a person to have an opinion about anything, it should follow that they have some knowledge of the subject. After all, imagine trying to critique a book you've never read, talk about a film you've never seen or describe a particular music style you've never heard.

Say that whatever pupils' reaction to Jesus is, you wonder how they came to have that opinion, and how much in fact they really know. Explain that you will have a quiz, pitching the boys against the girls. Choose two boys and two girls to act as spokespersons, but allow time after each question for some crowd involvement. Here are some suggested multiple choice style questions:

1. What was the name of Jesus' paternal grandfather?
   - (a) Joseph
   - (b) Jacob*
   - (c) Nigel

2. What was the name of the king who tried to kill Jesus as a baby?
   - (a) Herod*
   - (b) Pontius Pilate
   - (c) Richard III

3. Who baptised Jesus?
   - (a) Mark
   - (b) Luke
   - (c) John*

4. What was Jesus' first recorded miracle?
   - (a) Turning water into wine*

(b) Calming a storm

(c) Healing a blind leper

5. How did Jesus describe himself?

(a) As a good man

(b) As a prophet

(c) As the Son of God*

6. Of which faith was Jesus?

(a) Jewish*

(b) Hindu

(c) Christian

7. How long did Jesus spend on the cross?

(a) 6 hours*

(b) 12 hours

(c) 3 days

8. How old was Jesus thought to be when he died?

(a) 30

(b) 33*

(c) 36

You can make up your own questions if you prefer, or you can add to or subtract from these, depending on time. Try to make the quiz interesting and get the whole assembly involved, maybe by putting the questions onto big screens and creating some kind of fun score board.

Close by congratulating the winners and challenging people to think about how much they individually know.

TEACHING POINT: Do we know enough about Jesus and his claims?

BIBLE REFERENCE: John 3:16.

APPLICATION: Given the high stakes dependent on their response, do they think they know enough about the Christian message?

THE FLOATING NUT

KS3 KS4

THEMES: God, Jesus, reliance.

INTRODUCTION: This idea was given to me by a friend who uses it regularly. It's an illustration showing the Christian message of how we need to fully trust Jesus to keep us afloat, and has been used in various ways and forms over the years. The basic message is that without Christ we'll sink, or even if we just lean on him we'll sink. What we need to do is put him at the centre of our life.

The visual nature of the illustration may make it difficult to use in a very large assembly gathering (you'll need to use discretion on that), but the point is very clear and easy to remember. For younger pupils this is a difficult concept but the idea could be adapted.

YOU WILL NEED
- a clear tank of water
- a metal nut
- a polystyrene strip

OUTLINE: Open by recalling some amusing anecdote about sinking. It can be about sailing, swimming, a deflating dinghy—anything of the like will suffice. Remember that it's not only water you can sink in. I was once walking in the New Forest and, typical of me, I suddenly sank to my hips in the biggest pit of mud I've ever encountered! To make matters worse, I and the friend I was with started laughing so much we lost all strength and it took about five minutes before we calmed down enough to drag me out!

Go on to mention that the Bible has much to say about sinking and floating:

- Noah, under God's guidance, built an ark that floated against all odds.
- Jonah hastily exited a boat and sank to the bottom of the sea, only to be retrieved by a rather large fish.
- After Jesus famously and miraculously walked on water, Peter copied him. When he kept his eyes on Jesus he was fine, but when he looked down he began to sink.

Now show the illustration, explaining that it illustrates quite simply the Christian belief of trusting in Jesus. The nut represents us, in the big wide world, which is represented by the tank of water. On our own, we will sink! (Show this by dropping the nut into the water.) Now introduce Jesus, represented by the strip of polystyrene. People question the relevance of Jesus—they test him out, maybe by trying church, praying a bit, reading parts of the Bible or just leaning on him in times of trouble. (Show this by trying to balance the nut on the polystyrene. It might float for a bit, but eventually it will sink.)

Finally explain the Christian belief that to live our lives as God intended, we need to put Jesus at the centre of our lives, allowing him to guide all we do. (Illustrate this by threading the polystyrene strip through the nut, thus causing it to float.)

TEACHING POINT: Don't ignore or just lean on Jesus. Put him at the centre of your life.

BIBLE REFERENCE: Matthew 14:22–31.

APPLICATION: Close by explaining that Christians do not claim that putting Jesus at the centre of their lives is an insurance policy against anything bad happening, but there is the assurance that whatever does happen Christ will always be with you and in you.

THE PRIVILEGE OF PAIN

THEMES: Pain, the human body, creation.

INTRODUCTION: Beginning as a biology lesson, this illustration aims to get students thinking about the awesome design of the human body, with particular reference to its defence mechanisms.

I was recently reading a book about pain—why we have to experience it and why in many instances it is essential that we do feel it. Although we don't welcome pain, for obvious reasons, without it our lives would be more problematic.

YOU WILL NEED
- a visual display of the human body (picture, dummy or live dummy!)
- a knitting needle

OUTLINE: Open the assembly by asking how many students enjoy biology lessons. (This will doubtless receive a less than enthusiastic response!) Go on to say that many people believe the human body evolved from nothing over the course of millions of years, but Christian belief is that it was created by God and in his image.

Now using your visual aid, give some interesting facts about our bodies. Find out your own, or use some of these I got from my local reference library:

- If we joined all the blood vessels in our body together, they would stretch 100,000 km, or 2.5 times around the world.
- Our bodies have 650 muscles. To smile uses 15; to take a single step uses around 200.
- Our heart pumps around 9,000 litres of blood a day.
- Our lungs contain around 300 million air sacs.
- Our tongues have around 8,000 taste buds, each bud with 20–30 tasting cells. As we get older we lose some of these, hence many old people complain that food tastes bland!
- Just 12 weeks after conception, a baby's brain, heart and other parts are formed. It weighs just 18 g and is around 6.5 cm long.

Go on to say that however wonderful the human body is, one thing we don't like is to be in any kind of physical pain. We can all recall at some time or other being in excruciating physical pain, and wishing we didn't have to suffer. Here you can ask for some stories of various gruesome injuries or share one of your own about a burn, cut, break, etc.

Rather than being a bad thing, though, the pain threshold is another example of the brilliant complexity of the human body, acting as a kind of defence mechanism. Without pain to warn us of certain things we would be much worse off. For example, leprosy sufferers feel no pain and subsequently damage themselves because they don't feel any warning signs, and alcoholics, numbed of sensitivity, can die of exposure, unable to feel the freezing cold temperatures. Pain is the early warning signal that saves us from these things if it's working properly.

Now demonstrate how the body has areas that are more sensitive to pain than others. Take a knitting needle and prod it into different parts of yourself! (Warn the students not to try this at home, as you are a trained professional!)

- The heel. Because the heel is hard-wearing you can dig in the needle quite hard before feeling anything at all. The skin on the soles of our feet is the thickest on our body, for obvious reasons (approximately 5 mm thick).
- The tip of the finger. Explain that this is more sensitive and you will feel a dull sense of pain much more quickly.
- The eye. The mere mention of this will get a groan from the assembly! Obviously don't actually put the needle in your eye, but even gesturing towards doing it will make the hair stand up on the back of some students' neck. Incidentally, the skin on our eyelids is the thinnest on our body (approximately 0.5 mm thick). (Note: Pointing a needle to the eye may be controversial in some schools—less so if you are well known or a regular visitor.)

All of these show how the pain network helps us to live safe lives. Conclude by pressing home the point of how amazing the creation of the human body is.

TEACHING POINT: The awesome features of the human body.

BIBLE REFERENCE: Psalm 139:13–16.

APPLICATION: Considering how amazing the human body is, could this have resulted without a creator?

INDEX OF THEMES

INDEX OF THEMES

SCRIPTURE INDEX

Numbers in brackets refer to idea numbers not page numbers.

OLD TESTAMENT

GENESIS

EXODUS

JOSHUA

1 SAMUEL

PSALMS

100 Simple Bible Crafts

by Sue Price

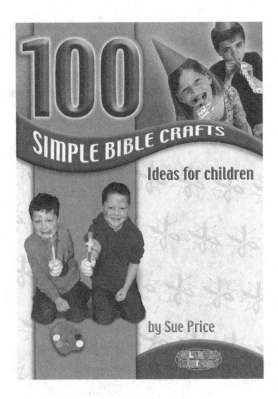

ISBN 978-1-84291-292-8

Many of us learn more effectively when we have something to see and something to make; when we interact rather than simply sit and listen. This collection of illustrated ideas has been specifically designed to help children learn stories and truths from the Bible in such a way that they can make them part of their lives. A useful resource that will prove invaluable to anyone who plays a part in the teaching of children.

50 Bible Dramas For Children

by Lynda Neilands

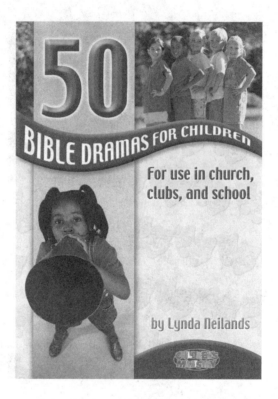

ISBN – 1 84291 253 4

These tried and tested dramas will help today's youngsters engage with the Bible. Not every drama is designed to be performed by children. Some will work better when adults perform them and others are written for a mixture of adult and child performers. At the start of each drama there is an indication of who should ideally perform the script. Each drama also has an application section with explore, chat and think ideas.

100 Children's Club Activities

by Jan Dyer

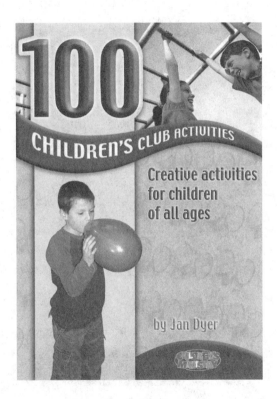

ISBN – 1 84291 289 5

More and more churches are discovering the importance of weekday or weekend children's clubs as a way to reach the families in their own local communities. This comprehensive volume features 100 creative activities for children of all ages and from a wide variety of cultural backgrounds, plus detailed guidelines on how to run a children's club, obtain the resources you need and make it a rewarding experience for all involved.

50 Five Minute Stories
by Lynda Neilands

ISBN – 1 84291 277 1

You have been asked to fill the next five or ten minutes. You want something that will hold the children's attention and stay in their minds. A story that will give the adults something to think about. You need fresh ideas, parables, true stories, once-upon-a-time stories. You need this book!

100 Instant Children's Talks
by Sue Relf

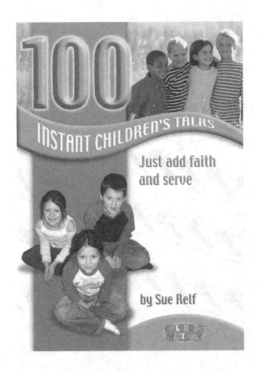

ISBN – 1 84291 290 9

Children's talks are needed to fit many situations – church services, family services, school assemblies, Bible clubs, holiday clubs and missions, regular children's activities and so on. Here are 100 ideas that can be fitted into all of these. The talks are not intended to be slavishly followed; they can be adapted, embellished, shortened, developed or altered in whatever way is necessary in order to make them suitable for the age and background of the children and the situation in which the talk is to be given.